Capital Market
Revolution

"When I started to work on Wall Street in 1970, average daily volume on the NYSE was just 11 million shares and IBM had a larger stock market capitalization than the entire Japanese stock market! Patrick Young is right when he writes about a Capital Market Revolution which will bring about dramatic changes deemed to be impossible just a few years ago. This is a thought-provoking and even scary book – because revolutions upset and destroy established orders. *Capital Market Revolution* is well worth a read for anyone who wants to understand how current developments and progress in capital markets will punctuate the economic equilibrium and lead to new winners and massive creative destruction of the old order."

Marc Faber, Editor of the "Gloom, Boom & Doom Report"

"It perhaps should have been called *The Rough Guide to Jericho*. This is not a subtle piece of writing that gently persuades one of the need to change. Rather, it very effectively screams, with all the compelling audacity of an Israelite trumpet, for the destruction of those traditional City walls."

Justin Urquhart Stewart, Corporate Development Director,
Barclays Stockbrokers

"*Capital Market Revolution* reads like a great Thomas Clancy high tech adventure novel that is nearly impossible to put down."

Trading on Target

"Patrick Young, [is] one of today's visionaries and realists concerning the future of the global finance industry."

Lisa Benjamin, Swiss Derivatives Review

Capital Market Revolution

The Future of Markets in an Online World

PATRICK YOUNG

WITH THOMAS THEYS

FINANCIAL TIMES

Prentice Hall

PEARSON EDUCATION LIMITED

Head Office:
Edinburgh Gate
Harlow CM20 2JE
Tel: +44 (0)1279 623623
Fax: +44 (0)1279 431059

London Office:
128 Long Acre, London WC2E 9AN
Tel: +44 (0)171 447 2000
Fax: +44 (0)171 240 5771
Website: www.business-minds.com

First published in Great Britain 1999

© Pearson Education Limited 1999

The Epilogue: The shape of things to come is © *Applied Derivatives Trading*,
(http://www.adtrading.com) 1998. Reproduced with permission.

The right of Patrick Young and Thomas Theys to be identified as authors
of this work has been asserted by them in accordance with the
Copyright, Designs, and Patents Act 1988.

ISBN 0 273 64232 4

British Library Cataloguing in Publication Data
A CIP catalogue record for this book can be obtained
from the British Library.

10 9 8 7 6 5 4

Typeset by Northern Phototypesetting Co. Ltd, Bolton.
Printed and bound in Great Britain by
Biddles Ltd, Guildford & King's Lynn.

The Publishers' policy is to use paper manufactured from sustainable forests.

About the Authors

Patrick Young is a professional trader and Editor of *Applied Derivatives Trading*, the unique Internet magazine that has readers in over 120 countries worldwide (http://www.adtrading.com). At the vanguard of the Capital Market Revolution, ADT has championed many radical visions for the future of financial markets ever since its launch in 1996. Born in Ireland, Young nowadays divides his time between Italy, Australia, and a multiplicity of hotel rooms on several continents in between. He is a regular conference speaker and acts as consultant to various banks and financial institutions. Away from the frenzy of trading, Young maintains a passion for classic cars.

Since leaving Chicago almost 20 years ago, **Thomas Theys** has been a long-standing independent ("local") trader on LIFFE in the UK apart from a year-long spell in Singapore at the inception of SIMEX. Driven by his belief in the future of electronic markets, Thomas founded Personal Automated Trading (PAT) Systems in 1996 to provide hand-held trading devices for floor dealers. Today, PATS is one of the largest front-end trading software suppliers, with terminals throughout the world.

This is for my mother, Joan, with all my love.
– Patrick Young

To my wife Patricia, who opened my eyes
in the mid '90s, telling me that my
days in the pit were numbered. And to
her patience with our struggles in
getting a new company off the ground …
Also to my late father-in-law, Ed Miller,
who believed in me every step of the way.
– Thomas Theys

In memoriam
Tony Webb, founding publisher of
Applied Derivatives Trading.
A great friend, a wonderful colleague,
and one of the original
Capital Market Revolutionaries.
– Patrick Young

CONTENTS

ACKNOWLEDGMENTS

The prospect of writing this book was at once exciting and intriguing. The project itself came to fruition through the melding of my ideas with an existing proposal to Financial Times Prentice Hall created by Beverly Chandler. To Beverly, both of us extend our thanks for creating the kernel of the idea that has grown into *Capital Market Revolution*.

Writing as it were from the front line of the revolutionary battlefield has undoubtedly made things difficult as the firmament was changing as fast as I could write about it. For instance, no sooner had I penned a – now expunged – chapter on the merits of merger between the Australian Stock Exchange and the Sydney Futures Exchange than rumours of merger talks between the two began to circulate! Nevertheless, this has been for me a most exciting project and one which I hope you will find suitably illuminating, concerning an upheaval that is simply so enormous in its ramifications as to be difficult to countenance. I can only hope that within these relatively slim covers we have given you sufficient inspiration to be able not merely to understand but also to survive and ultimately profit from the revolution.

Capital Market Revolution was written with some alacrity by myself, with input from Thomas Theys. I have known Thomas for several years and would like to thank him for the several nuggets he suggested in the text that have enhanced the book's "bite". Similarly, our publishers Richard Stagg, Iain Campbell and Martin Drewe have been a great help throughout this project, coping ably with my own need to write and rewrite great swathes of text with some alacrity. The staff at Financial Times Prentice Hall have done a great job coping with the editing of this book as not only was it written at breakneck speed but it has also been the subject of fine tuning by myself as the weeks ticked down to publication.

ACKNOWLEDGMENTS

On a personal note, this book would never have been completed without the great support from Denise Graham-Bowen who has put up with my frantic typing at all hours of the day and night, including throughout the Christmas and New Year holidays and other times when doubtless she would have welcomed some attention. Similarly, the late Tony Webb was always an indomitable business partner in both the overlap of our consulting/ training business and also with *Applied Derivatives Trading* (http://www.adtrading.com). Moreover, Steve Black has been a tireless supporter of *ADT* and indeed it was he who first referred to the concept of the "New Reality". My thanks to Steve for allowing us to use his phrase and also for permission to reproduce the Epilogue, "The shape of things to come" which he contributed to *ADT*.

On my roving travels a number of folk have generously provided accommodation, Internet access, and sustenance during the genesis of this book. In particular, I would like to thank my very good friends Charles Sidey and Gabby Leiders who are amongst London's most generous hosts. I owe them both a huge debt for allowing *Capital Market Revolution* to dominate their living room in manuscript form for several weeks. Thanks also must go to Harry and Ann Graham, Jeff, Sharmaine, Alf Guadagnino, and Ruth for putting up with what has undoubtedly been an entirely self-absorbed houseguest on occasion.

Throughout the writing of *Capital Market Revolution*, I have been delighted to call upon various very good friends who have been happy to while away many an hour informing me of areas of their specialist technological expertise or debating the finer points of the New Reality. In particular, Rory Collins has been a complete star with endless piercing insights and amusing anecdotes. My dear friends Jeremy and Julie Braithwaite have been hugely supportive and enthusiastic about this project from its birth and their unstinting forwarding of appropriate cuttings is greatly appreciated, even if Jeremy is still faster than me at Grand Prix 2 and simply beyond compare at Grand Prix Legends!

While it pains me to include a mere list given their input into the project, alas even to remotely acknowledge everybody who has helped with *Capital Market Revolution* would probably occupy a fairly healthily sized paperback tome in its own right. Therefore, a representative selection follows with the caveat that my gratitude is no less to others omitted from this list.

Anyway, my thanks therefore (in alphabetical order) go to: Bob Aalam, Michael Aikins, Gwen Aimee, Walter Allwicher, Jarrid Anderson, Jim Austin, Graham Ayre, Mamdouh Barakat, Cosima Barone, Antoinette Bouvier-Darpy, Lesley Boxall, Brendan Bradley, Phil Bruce, Xavier Bruckert, Bill Burnham, Alex Carpenter, Mike Charlton, Raymond Cheseldine, David Chin, Sean Coakley, Richard Cook, Will Corry, Bob Cotton, Peter Cox, Phil Cramp, Joe Cross, David Dancox, Paul Davis, Brian Davison, Gary Delany, Caroline Denton, Robert Dischel, Bill Doyle, Matt Docherty, Danielle Dycus, Marc Faber, Stuart Frith, Sir Peter Froggatt, Richard Froggatt, David Ganis, Alan Genn, Luca Giovannetti, Grant Graham, Lewis Graham, Lindsay Graham, Sammy Graham, Olivier Gueris, Kristina Halvarsson, Noriko Hama, Richard Hanson, Chris Hartley, James Henry, John Herron, John Hinge, Martin Hollander, Fiona Hoppe, Bernard Horn, Rachel Horn, Shirley Horn, Daniel Jones, Katie Jones, Michael de Kantzow, Jack Kelly, Andrew Klein, George Kleinman, Seana Lanigan, Jim Lee, Andre Lewis, Luca Lombardo, John Mackeonis, Jeff Marsh, Sean Matthews, Janelle McKimm, Sophie Melcion, Kieran Moffat, Olivier de Montety, Philip Nixon, Mike O'Hara, Marlene Panholzer, Peter Panholzer, John Parry, Juliette Proudlove, Arthur Rabatin, Geoff Reynolds, Angus Richards, Laura Rigby, Paul Ritchie, Clive Roberts, Maruska Rood, Riccardo Ronco, Simon Rostron, Gustaf Sahlman, Pascal Samaran, Dr. Richard Sandor, Emily Saunderson, the ladies of the SFE library, Guy Simpkin, Jean-Yves Sireau, Carol Spagg, Mike Stiller, Rob Sucher, Mark Thornberry, Luellen Triltsch, Liz Valentine, Tim Van Doorn, Suzanne Wallace, Linda Walrad, Colin Walsh, Lucie Wang, Max Whitby, Velta Whyte, Brian Williamson, Liz Wilson and Steve Zwick.

In addition, Thomas wishes to thank his parents, Jim and June Theys, and mother-in-law, Sue Miller, along with: Larry Arnowitz,

John Asgian, Charlie Barwis, Iain Bell, Santiago Benede, Dave Brennan, Ed Cashman, Mandie Downie, Scott Franklin, Jim Froelich, Roberto and Paola Giovanelli, Peter Green, Steve Harrigan, Paul Hayward, Nicky Hickman, David Kyte, Howard Lutnick, Harvey Moses, Larry Nocek, Jose-Luis Oller, Dave Page, Jerry Rodgers, Mark and John Stanton, Noel Starbuck and Joe Theys.

To everybody who has assisted in the creation of *Capital Market Revolution*, my thanks to you all.

Patrick Young, Perinaldo, Italy, May 1999

FOREWORD

"Economic history is the story of the gradual extension of the economic community beyond its original limits of the single household to embrace the nation and the world."

Ludwig Von Mises, *The Theory of Money and Credit*

Moore's Law, bandwidth, packet loss, APIs, GUIs, and a score of other terms and acronyms at first sight provide professional traders with a dense picture of the brave new world of electronic trading. However, it is possible to write a clear and readable book on what these terms mean and the implications for market participants. If you are a skeptic just continue to turn the pages of *Capital Market Revolution*. This book looks at the way the world is changing and how these changes in an online world will affect those of us who work in markets.

In the decade of the 1960s, futures trading had been undergoing subtle but important changes – with the extension of trading from primary commodities to semiprocessed and fully processed commodities as well as live animals.

The decade of the 1970s witnessed the beginning of the largest transformation in the history of futures markets, and perhaps world monetary and capital markets, with the introduction of interest rate and currency futures. These developments had their counterparts in the equity markets with the emergence of exchange-traded equity options.

The 1980s began a second wave of innovation in futures markets with the inception of trading in options on futures, stock index futures, and the extension of futures trading to time zones throughout the world. New interest rate and equity derivatives were introduced throughout the decade and exchanges began proliferating in every continent.

The dramatic change in the landscape is easily demonstrated by looking at two points in time. In 1975 there were four main exchanges in the United States that traded interest rate derivatives, currency derivatives and equity options. The Chicago Board of Trade, the Chicago Mercantile Exchange, the Chicago Board of Options Exchange, the American Stock Exchange and a few others had a combined volume of roughly 18 million contracts, mainly in stock options. By 1995 there were in excess of 50 exchanges worldwide with a volume of over 1.8 billion contracts.

The decade of the 1990s would usher in the era of the next major revolution in markets – electronic trading. The seeds had been planted earlier. The first efforts in this area occurred in the late 1960s at the University of California, Berkeley, where a group of economists, electrical engineers and programmers researched the feasibility of an electronic exchange.[1] The author of this foreword had the privilege of being the team leader. However, the necessary technology wasn't available. It was too early. The Bermuda Exchange was second to try – once again, too early. Then in the late 1980s the Chicago Mercantile Exchange began an after-hours market that would ultimately prove successful. Its counterpart, Project A at the Chicago Board of Trade, would become an even bigger success. However, both these markets were only after-hours facilities and couldn't lead the way to full scale electronic markets. It would take initial efforts by a small Swedish Exchange, OM, and ultimately the German Exchange, Deutsche Terminbörse, to lead the markets into the brave new world. Eurex's success has been extraordinary, but the work of the computer nerds has only just begun. In the immortal words of the Hollywood producer (Dustin Hoffman) in the film 'Wag the Dog', "This is nothing" – a statement that can easily be seen as the off-hand remarks of the technophile revolutionaries in an online trading world. But why didn't these innovations take place on the existing open outcry exchanges in the United States and England? What were the political forces and market economics that powered innovation in Germany?

Capital Market Revolution provides a highly readable narrative on the circumstances surrounding the birth of electronic markets in an online world. It is a colorful account of the demise of open outcry in Europe and its precarious position in the United States. C. Northcote Parkinson, author of the eponymous law, points out that the decline in capital ships in commission in the British Navy between 1914 and 1928 was accompanied by a similar percentage increase in Admiralty officials.[2] Exchanges, as mutual forms of organizations operating in regulated environments, seem to obey Parkinson's law. Committees proliferate and regulatory and exchange staffs expand. They suffer from injelititis, or a sense of paralysis. Patrick Young and Thomas Theys understand this and convey it to the reader in a thoroughly enjoyable manner. They describe how the open outcry markets celebrated themselves at the height of their success with grand anniversary parties. They built brick and mortar structures as opposed to spending on technology, in the middle of the greatest transformation in economics since the industrial revolution. What is even more important than understanding the demise of open outcry in Europe is the insight the authors bring to the nature of futures markets in an online world. Their description of the changing value proposition and the New Reality are provocative. Exchanges, traders and brokers, like Madonna and other celebrities, will have to reinvent themselves.

This book provides a roadmap into the value chain in an electronic world. This brave new world will certainly change the nature of what is already an innovative industry. Rather than stifling the growth of these businesses their opportunities are boundless. The seventh stage of market development, where deconstruction occurs, will be facilitated in an online world.[3] While the challenges of the past dictated the invention of a homogeneous instrument such as bond or stock index futures, attention can now be turned to the development of hundreds or even thousands of new products that deconstruct these indices into components that can cost-effectively be traded electronically. For example, in a highly segmented market such as the U.S. market in wholesale electricity, a single price index is not meaningful or necessary. Multiple regional indices could be traded. The applications are enormous. Thousands of new products can easily be envisioned in not only electricity but also in weather, insurance, credit, and even bandwidth. This electronic age might generate its own new products based on bandwidth, routing and the new information economy. We are already witnessing these changes with the emergence of entertainment derivatives.

The electronic and virtual worlds, coupled with the information economy, may generate new goods and services which none of us can imagine. All these unborn products may ultimately become online markets. The statement of the neoclassical Austrian economist, Ludwig Von Mises, 100 years ago, seems prescient. His hypothesis will be taken to its logical conclusion in the online and virtual reality world of tomorrow. This book will help guide readers into their place in this new wired world.

Richard L. Sandor
Chairman and CEO, Environmental Financial Products,
Visiting Scholar at Northwestern University,
Senior Advisor to PricewaterhouseCoopers

Notes

1 "West Coast looks to the futures", *Financial Times*, 25 June, 1970.
2 C. Northcote Parkinson, *Parkinson's Law and Other Studies in Administration*. First ed. (Boston: Houghton Mifflin, 1957).
3 Richard L. Sandor, "The role of the United States in international environmental policy" in *Preparing America's Foreign Policy for the Twenty-first Century*. Eds. David L. Boren and Edward J. Perkins (Norman: University of Oklahoma Press, 1999), 253–66.

U.S. COMMODITY MARKETS

West Coast looks to the futures

BY A SPECIAL CORRESPONDENT

THE western United States, which has never had a commodities exchange, suddenly has plans underway for two of them, one to be located in San Francisco, the other in Los Angeles ...

In San Francisco, a proposed Pacific Commodities Exchange has been incorporated and recently received an initial go-ahead in a feasibility report prepared by the University of California. The preliminary report, commissioned by the newly-formed Pacific Commodities Exchange Inc., states that a computerised exchange dealing in western and Pacific region commodities is both economically and technically feasible ...

The commodity exchange of the kind the University of California is studying would be the first to be fully computerised. It could operate 24 hours a day, seven days a week, with traders working from office or home through a telecommunication system linked with other similar setups to a central computer.

The California Commodity Advisory and Research Project that is making the study is administered by the Institute of Business and Economic Research at the University of California's Berkeley campus. Professor Richard Sandor, project director, sees a western U.S. commodities exchange as possibly "the exchange of the future." He envisages no pit, ring or trading floor but an exchange hooked up by a "vast communication network," computers, split-second automatic execution of buy-sell orders, and poised for the 144m. commodities trading-volume-year he predicts over the next 30 years ...

"It's a rather mind-expanding project," he adds, "A computer can work 24 hours a day. If this system could work, why not trade foreign exchange and bankers' acceptances?"

The Financial Times,
Thursday 25 June, 1970

INTRODUCTION

Nowhere to hide, nowhere to run

"Explaining the new way of doing computers and networks is difficult. It's like expecting people in a feudal society to know what it would be like to live in a capitalistic society. It's just too hard to imagine until you're in it."

Bill Toy, Sun Microsystems

There is nowhere to hide from capital markets. Nobody is safe from the Capital Market Revolution. The Capital Market Revolution presents the greatest upheaval ever seen in the fabric of financial markets, and is born of, and driven by, new technology which will ultimately change the lives of every individual on the globe.

Exchanges thought new technology would secure their future through wider product bases and increased access to their products. Institutions saw it as a means to create great economies of scale in ever larger multinational frameworks. Brokers saw computerization as a means to bolster pressurized margins. Instead, the power of information technology threatens to destroy them all. That, very simply is the message of the Capital Market Revolution.

No broker, no banker, no middleman can count their position as being safe from the revolution. This is not an uprising that will bring the masses on to the streets to ensure it occurs. However, this is a revolution so profound in its global consequences for every single man, woman and child on Earth that it can (and likely will) bring masses on to the streets within a decade to overthrow the large lumbering government bureaucracies that have failed to appreciate the paradigm shift in world finance.

Revolutionaries, Reactionaries or Luddites?

Throughout the text of this book, we will refer to those espousing the Capital Market Revolution as revolutionaries and those who are against it as Luddites. Why not reactionaries? Well, reaction suggests a mild-mannered viewpoint becoming of country gentlemen and Christian Democrat politicians – a response which is normally not vastly harmful but not greatly beneficial either. In the Capital Market Revolution, those seeking to uphold the status quo, or even vaguely tinker with it, will be trampled underfoot with their arguments against electronic markets forming a barely audible whisper. This revolution will simply blow reactionaries away. Any person or organization eschewing the attitudes, attributes and skill sets required for the digital trading revolution, or even aspiring very gently to set the clock back, will be forced out of positions at the heart of the financial markets.

Therefore, as reactionaries are too mild to sustain any opposition to the dynamic forces of the Capital Market Revolution, we have chosen to refer to those more fiercely opposed to the whole process as Luddites. Ned Ludd is a semi-mythical character who is reputed to have broken into a factory in Nottingham at around the turn of the nineteenth century and who (according to the Oxford English Dictionary) "in a fit of insane rage" destroyed two knitting machines. As word spread about Ludd's actions, all such acts of industrial age vandalism were greeted with the phrase "Ludd must have been here." Bands of Luddites flourished in Britain from about 1811 until 1816. Groups of masked men swore allegiance to "King Ludd" and destroyed textile machinery. Therefore, for the purposes of this book, we will employ the term "Luddite" as our preferred method of describing those of a counter-revolutionary persuasion. Of course we're not suggesting that all those disbelieving in the Capital Market Revolution will seek to destroy the computer apparatus at its core, but we do feel such counter-revolutionaries will actively attempt to thwart the progress of the revolution.

Although its origins are in technology, the Capital Market Revolution is most certainly not a simple tale of markets being enveloped by a raft of computer screens that make financial markets easier for existing counterparties to transact business. Rather, the revolution is a genuine paradigm shift in the processes of financial markets that can completely alter not just how financiers interact but how the public at large can actually participate in financial markets with more influence than ever before in history. The core issue is not how the playing field will operate in the next millennium but rather what the playing field will be.

> "The Internet is the Gutenburg press on steroids. Gutenberg wasn't about how many bibles were printed, but the fact that you no longer had to listen to the clerics."
>
> **Watts Wacker, consultant and resident futurist, SRI International Upside**

This is a revolution in financial markets that will change the world. Since Gutenberg revolutionized the business of printing in the fifteenth century, markets and media have traditionally operated from a single standpoint disseminating via a network (covering increasing distances as distribution has been perfected). However, digital media now make multiple access and dissemination from any point to any other point possible. This multivariable access and dissemination structure will ultimately undermine current market structures which are rooted in a handful of big cities.

There have been many times when the system of open outcry has been written off as an anachronism, although all have proven incorrect – until now. None of the telecommunications innovations of the late nineteenth and early twentieth century hampered trading on exchanges in financial centers. Rather it expressly aided them. The invention of telegraph and later telex, telephone and fax, merely facilitated traders from further and further away being able to deal straight to the marketplace in question. The tyranny of distance to the market was reduced, if not quite removed altogether, making the trading process more accessible to all.

In the modern marketplace, the obvious threat to open outcry comes from the entire technological revolution driven by the microchip. Gordon Moore, the founder of leading chip manufacturer Intel, made a startling (some would have said hysterical) statement in 1965 when he posited "Moore's Law" that computer processing power would double every 18 months. The accuracy of his prophecy, still being proven three decades later is uncanny. The compound result is that computer processing is now so fast and powerful that it can threaten the established open outcry financial markets.

The increasing growth in computing power and the widespread popularization of systems such as the Internet mean that information can now be sent from anywhere to anywhere, creating a whole new playing field. In the past, financial information has traditionally been freely available only to the richest and most powerful individuals and corporations on planet Earth. Before Gutenberg, literacy was limited to a tiny proportion of society, most notably nobility and employees of the church. When the printing press was invented it didn't merely level the playing field to make information more freely available to all levels of society, rather it revolutionized society by providing a new, cheap method of disseminating information to far more people than could be accommodated by the handwritten copying of manuscripts in monasteries. In the information age the Internet provides the opportunity to pass on vast quantities of information at little incremental cost to every form of trader, investor, and market counterparty. The old hegemony of existing institutional investors, exchanges, and brokers is doomed to collapse under the "New Reality." Just as the clerics lost power after Gutenburg, the information revolution undermines the power of established financial institutions.

Bankers must become bionic or be bypassed.

Moreover, the Internet has removed the tyranny of distance from communication. Investment can now be undertaken from anywhere to anywhere at the click of a mouse. This aspect of the information revolution means that the New Reality will affect not only market counterparties and mechanisms but also the regulators and indeed the future well-being of government finances throughout the world. If any of these groupings fails to reform in line with the precepts of the New Reality, they will find themselves out of business. Bankers must become bionic or be bypassed.

Existing financial markets are under the most concerted threat in their history from new technologies. The modified modalities of trading will create whole new online communities exerting similar mercantile might to the medieval city states. From foreign exchange markets to swaps trading, the entire marketplace is changing. Equally, the lower cost of entry to the electronic marketplace threatens the very existence of not merely existing financial intermediaries but indeed the very markets that have operated uninterrupted in centers like Amsterdam and London for hundreds of years.

"Exchanges really are a rather low form of life. There is a tendency to look at exchanges as one of three things: as a utility, as an institution, or even, God forbid, as part of the social fabric. Rather, the business of the exchange is high yield, low value. The exchange is a servant of markets."

Brian Williamson, Executive Chairman, LIFFE

The most frequent problem with all types of large financial institutions has been their apparent ivory tower mentality. Exchanges became sacrosanct in the late twentieth century. Their status as revered demi-gods of financial markets is now far too perilous for them to survive without radical change. Too many high-ranking managers have spent too long trying to avoid the fray from the comfort of management offices, rather than trying to get into the trenches alongside their members and assess what they really require. The more brokerage rates fall, the less brokers are able to offer a good full-service operation.

As we will examine presently, in almost every section of society, the business of technology is being driven from the USA. Indeed, on equity markets, the National Association of Securities Dealers Automated Quotation system (NASDAQ) has become a leviathan in securities trading, especially amongst high-technology stocks. However, when the USA (and indeed the world) think of stocks and shares, they visualize the frenzied activity on Wall Street at the New York Stock Exchange. Despite a number of interesting innovations that we will address in later chapters, in the main the new technology ethos for dealing processes is being driven by derivatives markets and in the main driven from Europe. This is all the more remarkable given the relatively statist and inflexible economics of much of Europe. Nevertheless, the fact remains that Europe is at the center of new market development as the world begins the new millennium. Thanks to the large concentration of foreign banks within the fabled "Square Mile," the City of London was first to encounter the dynamic processes of the Capital Market Revolution. On foreign turf, banks could afford to be more promiscuous. The revolution hit LIFFE (London International Financial Futures and Options Exchange) so hard as to leave the exchange reeling and questioning the viability of its existence within months of briefly becoming the largest market on Earth. While the German-Swiss EUREX exchange was the hot market in the late 1990s, with stunning volume increases, the fact remained that even as it won the key German Bond (Bund) futures contract from LIFFE, the increased promiscuity of screen dealing itself threatens the future well-being of the Frankfurt-based market. EUREX became the biggest exchange in the world early in 1999. Yet it will need to move fast to maintain this position in the midst of a revolution which it largely fuelled but which may yet engulf its original proponents.

Capital Market Revolution reviews successively the factors behind the revolution and the likely impacts upon not merely the established markets and intermediaries but also the individual players who will shape the new markets. Indeed, the Capital Market Revolution will shape not merely a new meritocracy but will also be driven by the irresistible rise of private capital investment that increasingly moves away from existing fund managers to be controlled by private individuals themselves. The markets of the future are markets where individual sovereignty is greater than has been witnessed in financial markets for many decades, if not centuries. The new meritocracy delivers power to the people in a way that was never achieved by any socialist model. Nevertheless, the rewards of prosperity from the Capital Market Revolution will be difficult to attain. To this end, we outline a series of key survival skills for all existing and budding brokers, traders, and other financial market personnel and practitoners in Chapter 9.

The status quo is not dead. Rather, there is no status quo. *Capital Market Revolution* seeks to outline the likely future for financial markets with equanimity. Therefore, readers may find some of the possible outcomes disturbing. Like any revolution, the Capital Market Revolution will not be a clean, simple, and easy-to-master process of progressive change. Rather, it will be an ongoing chaotic process that will create haves and have-nots, often stripping away centuries of financial achievement from individual dynasties, institutions and even sovereign states.

> **The status quo is not dead. Rather, there is no status quo.**

In many respects, clearing houses hold the aces for the new millennium. Like feudal princes in medieval times, they have the opportunity to wield power over which new model exchanges retain financial credibility. Exchanges will struggle and many will die but clearing houses are entering their most influential era yet. Nevertheless, not everything is golden even here. The possibility of netting clearing and better collateralization procedures on the over-the-counter (OTC) markets does pose a significant threat to the largest institutional businesses which may remain reluctant to come under the clearing houses's remit. Many of the biggest bulge-bracket banks question why, given their titanic size, they have to post any form of margin against their trades, least of all at the same prevailing rates as are applied uniformly by the clearing house to everybody from the largest multinational institutions to the smallest one-lot traders.

> **There are no more gentlemen and the players are dying. In the future there will only be electronic traders.**

There are no more gentlemen and the players are dying. In the future there will only be electronic traders. All the revolutionary processes are gradually gaining pace in financial markets and no government or governmental body will be able to do anything but acknowledge the power of the marketplace to adjudicate how good a job they are doing. The US Securities and Exchange Commission (SEC) is already desperately endeavoring to keep its mandate to regulate. Other nations of the world are demonstrating a characteristic bureaucratic heavy-handedness which will leave their countries years behind the cyber elite.

The authors make no apologies for the fact that their conclusions may in many cases be unpalatable to many individuals and corporations. However, financial markets have always been engines of change, driving processes to create change. Now, the Capital Market Revolution is in a position to rework every single established factor about financial markets which everyday investors take for granted.

Given their pedigree as both floor and off-floor traders, as brokers, advisers, and consultants to a diverse range of corporations and markets worldwide, the authors feel they are qualified to provide a unique insight into the future of world markets. *Capital Market Revolution* is a book which we hope will outline not just a sensible blueprint for future financial markets and their practitioners (both at an individual and a macro level) but also provide a helpful handbook for the future of finance in an online world. In keeping with our belief in openness and transparency in financial markets, we welcome feedback from all readers using the appropriate e-mail addresses below.

In the meantime, we hope you will enjoy our journey through the financial markets at this most exciting juncture and remember the key slogan of the Capital Market Revolution: "Liquidity! Accessibility! Transparency!" Markets which operate in accordance with this maxim will find themselves in the best position to survive and prosper in the Capital Market Revolution.

Patrick Young <PLY@adtrading.com>
Thomas Theys <TTheys@PATSystems.com>

PROLOGUE: GENESIS OF A REVOLUTION

"Open outcry has survived every other innovation in history."

Bob Wilmouth, President, NFA (National Futures Association of the USA)

"It is only a matter of time before all financial instruments can be traded electronically."

Charles Sidey, Managing Director, OF Broking Ltd, London

London, 4 June, 1997: An almost indiscernible chill wind of discontent had been growing for some time. Nevertheless, the status quo still looked assured as Daniel Hodson entered the ballroom at the Intercontinental hotel, in the heart of Mayfair. Hodson, the CEO of the London International Financial Futures Exchange, was riding high. LIFFE was celebrating its 15th birthday with the news that it was now the second largest derivatives market on the planet. The long-time stranglehold on futures and options trading held by the Chicago exchanges had finally been broken, by a European interloper over a hundred years younger than either of the American markets. While the derivatives business had experienced massive growth in the previous decade, the established order had always shown the hegemony to favour the Chicago Board of Trade and the Chicago Mercantile Exchange, neighboring monoliths dominating the exchange traded landscape. Now LIFFE had split the duopoly.

London's International Derivatives Week is an established event on the global financial calendar. Leading figures from all aspects of derivatives markets attend exhibitions, conferences and receptions scattered across the Square Mile and the West End. Syon House, the Seat of the Dukes of Northumberland, would host the highlight of LIFFE's 15th anniversary celebrations. In the Tudor Mansion with interiors remodeled by Robert Adam, to the south-west of central London, the conclusion of Futures Week was a sumptuous Gala Ball for some 3,500 of the world's leading traders and financial notables.

Invitations had become hot currency in the week leading up to the event. In the multi-billion dollar global derivative business, hundreds of traders in London and further afield would be disappointed at being left without an invitation to the elite gathering. Brokers were scrambling to beg, borrow and steal tickets for key clients, while stories of journalists haranguing the LIFFE press office to secure an invitation were not unknown …

Throughout the week, Hodson was at the very epicenter of the celebrations, as the man who had helped shape the exchange in its most recent years of dynamic growth. Surpassing the Chicago Mercantile Exchange had been an achievement universally regarded as impossible only a few years earlier. Now, LIFFE had the world's number one exchange, the Chicago Board of Trade, firmly in its sights, even surpassing the CBOT for one fleeting month during early 1997. Many might have felt the future lay with electronic dealing but Hodson was in the vanguard of supporting the historic open outcry methods, involving pits containing colorfully jacketed traders shouting at one another.

The centerpiece of the joint FIA/FOA conference[1] held during London Futures Week was a debate sponsored by Reuters with polling via hand-held terminals courtesy of the UK-based multinational news and information giant. Enthusiastically chairing the motion, "This House Believes That Floor Trading Will Not Survive The Challenge Of New Technology", was Christopher Sharples, the Chairman of ICV Datastream, a major technologically-oriented data vendor. An initial vote ahead of hostilities starting gave the motion a stunning 75 per cent support level, while a mere 25 per cent felt that floor trading held the best cards for the future.

Undaunted by this vote against the core *modus operandi* of the LIFFE exchange, Daniel Hodson rose to oppose the motion with the air of a man who knew he had everything going for him. In an impassioned speech "dapper Dan", as one derivatives publication dubbed him, spoke as if his life depended on winning this debate. While his first core point (to always distrust motions containing hyperbole) bore all the hallmarks of an English public school attitude to debate, Hodson went on to exhort the audience to "always remember that technology is far from an opponent to open outcry, rather it is a friend of open outcry." Hodson emphasized the human dimension and advantage of open outcry trading: "No electronic trading system will be able to replicate the advantages of open outcry." Indeed, the human factor was key to making floor trading more flexible, more liquid and better at "price discovery" than electronic alternatives.

Moreover, the LIFFE CEO added, reliability is an omnipresent concern for derivatives markets. Unlike computers, "people don't collectively fall over or work slowly" – a barbed reference to German rival the Deutsche Terminbörse (DTB) which was suffering frequent bouts of unreliability. Concluding his rousing address with a flourish, Hodson added, "With floor trading, it is technology which will ensure its continued existence."

Despite Hodson's formidable reputation in debate, the proposition had not merely rolled over and played dead. Ros Wilton, a former Drexel Burnham Lambert supremo and now MD of transaction products at the information business's foremost name, Reuters PLC, had made some crushing points for the proposition, such as "Technology is the only way to consistently grow this business economically." Playing on the fears of hard-pressed brokers, she added: "Commissions are going down while costs are rising … somebody must bear the costs associated with open outcry." Acknowledging the emotional nature of the debate, Wilton's final point in favour of electronic transactions was, "I know it's the fairest method of trading."

Seconding the proposition, Bruce Pollock, a director of BWO Bank in Switzerland ridiculed the old-fashioned nature of face to face "open outcry" dealing, by likening it to an outmoded period piece, such as a horse and buggy. Very pretty, very interesting, but outmoded compared to contemporary alternatives. Emphasizing Ros Wilton's clarion call, he added, "I love open outcry, but it doesn't make good economic sense."

Carl Boraiko, a former Chicago trader now resident in London as a local on the LIFFE floor, bolstered Daniel Hodson's arguments. Boraiko noted that, with the advancement of technology, screen trading gave more opportunity for front running.[2] The much vaunted electronic audit trails only began when a trade was entered into the computer system. If counterparties so desired, there was nothing to prevent them from pre-arranging trades before input.[3]

Cost, Boraiko agreed, was an over-riding factor in brokerage companies' considerations. However, electronic trading's cost advantage was unlikely to emerge if screen trading developed. There would be increasing customer demand for individual screens, with their own personalized traders and order teams which, combined, would inflate the overall costs involved with screen trading, and so fail to provide the cost benefits often claimed for the move to electronic dealing.

On open outcry markets, he commented, "we embrace technology in just the same way as electronic markets embrace technology." He concluded, "I could continue to expose the electronic markets for what they are – amateurs trying to compete with the pros" and cautioned the house to recall that locals (independent traders risking their personal capital to facilitate trade on exchange floors) are a source of human input and a major source of liquidity. Boraiko could not see why such locals would wish to switch to electronic markets.

When the debate was open to the floor, Bob Wilmouth was first to speak. The sexagenerian President of the NFA (National Futures Association of the USA) was firmly in opposition to the motion. Business flow to the best and most liquid market was vital to him: "Open outcry has survived every other innovation in history."

Meanwhile, almost all aspects of the possibilities provided by new technology were covered from the floor participants. Richard Jacobs of Computer Trading Corporation raised the spectre of virtual reality. He felt that open outcry would always exist, although ultimately it would be in an electronic format.

In his concluding remarks, an ebullient Daniel Hodson maintained his crushing form, noting that, "Open outcry will survive and it won't just be in Managua or Bangkok." Despite the excellent speeches from the proposition, the end result hinged on Hodson's bravura performance ... indeed, when the numbers appeared on the screen behind the Chairman's head, the final vote brought a collective gasp from the crowd with the votes having moved to only 57 percent for the motion (down from an initial 75 percent) and 43 percent against.

As the Internet magazine *Applied Derivatives Trading* noted at the time:

"Was it a victory, perhaps pyrrhic, for the battling brilliance of the excellent Daniel Hodson? Or was it, as some electronic trading officials muttered darkly, evidence of lurking open outcry supporters employing tactical voting – initially hiding their genuine feelings, only to reveal them on the second vote. Whatever, the real result will doubtless take some years to become apparent ..."

In fact, the real result became apparent much, much sooner. A little over 13 months later, on 21 July 1998, Daniel Hodson resigned as LIFFE CEO. Chairman Jack Wigglesworth had already stood down. At least Wigglesworth had a job to go back to. Deputy Chairman Chris Hartley found himself both resigning and also out of a job as head of futures brokerage at Dean Witter (due to the Morgan Stanley Dean Witter merger) all within a matter of weeks.[4]

In a frenzied period of months, the LIFFE exchange had, as Edward Luce described it in the *FT*, "undergone a road-to-Damascus conversion to electronic trading." In addition to seeking to dump open outcry in favor of electronic trading mechanisms, the London market launched a wholesale dumping of core principles. LIFFE demutualized its member-owned structure in favor of becoming a profit-seeking business. There were mass sackings. In the exchange's day of the long knives, at a hastily convened press conference on Monday 2 November, LIFFE announced that 600 employees out of over 1,000 would be made redundant, in addition to an earlier freezing in new staff.

When the first sackings took place, a few hours after being axed one bewildered former manager stated, "I thought I was okay but then I got called in on the third wave." In management terms, it all sounded akin to the trench-emptying tactics of British generals at the Battle of the Somme. Not for nothing was the new LIFFE CEO, Hugh Freedburg, described by one unnamed former colleague at Hill Samuel as "the man who put the slash into 'slash and burn.'"

However, with 98 percent of the LIFFE membership voting for electronic trading in an Extraordinary General Meeting (EGM) on May 12th, 1998, the new Executive Chairman, Brian Williamson, had received the mandate he required to make sweeping changes at the very heart of the derivatives business. Open outcry may have survived every other innovation in history, but time had finally caught up with it.

The Capital Market Revolution had claimed its highest profile victims to date …

Notes

1 The FOA is the UK Futures and Options Association, the FIA is the larger and older Futures Industry Association of the USA – respectively the two largest industry groups in the derivatives trading business.
2 "Front Running" refers to counterparties entering orders ahead of large client trades, perhaps the ultimate sin a broker can commit
3 "Pre-arranging" trades before they reach an exchange mechanism is a heinous crime in trading.
4 Hartley subsequently found a new position as an Executive Director – Client Relations, at Warburg Dillon Read.

CHAPTER 1

The death of open outcry

Information technology defeats the establishment

> "Worldwide, once confident, even arrogant, futures exchanges face a fast-mounting challenge to their primacy."
>
> **Robert Clow, *Institutional Investor Magazine***

Why open outcry died

The origin of the Capital Market Revolution lies many years ago. In the beginning, dealing was in small localized markets, but with the birth of telecommunications, exchanges migrated to larger centers. With the development of the Internet and the explosion in computer technology during the late 1990s, the world's financial makets were poised for the greatest upheaval in their history. The landmark event demonstrating to the public at large that the Capital Market Revolution was already well under way took place in early 1999: the Chicago Board of Trade was overtaken as the world's largest futures exchange by the entirely digital Germano-Swiss EUREX, headquartered in Frankfurt. For EUREX it was a bittersweet victory being crowned futures "world champions" over the heads of the American market which, having lamely grasped the concepts behind the Capital Market Revolution in late 1998, had eventually opted out of an alliance agreement with the European electronic market only weeks before. For the CBOT to be so comprehensively surpassed in trading volume was an event, in the financial world, with huge revolutionary repercussions.

Electronic trading had swung to global prominence in October 1997 when the German Deutsche Terminbörse (DTB) – soon to be merged with Switzerland's SOFFEX to create EUREX – first broke through a 50 percent volume share on the key German Bund futures contracts, which had previously been dominated by LIFFE. The winds of change blew through London first, largely because it is the most cosmopolitan of all the world's financial centers. Foreign banks can afford to be more promiscuous than local banks as the latter will always have greater customer and political problems if they are seen to be removing their business from the local economy. Foreign banks can largely act with impunity away from their home markets. In London, much of the deal making and trading capacity is created by these foreign banks thanks to the cosmopolitan history of the "Square Mile", London's financial district. Thus it was that the battle of the Bund was resolved by foreign banks moving their business to Frankfurt in preference for electronic systems cheaper than the existing floor trading system in London. In many ways the EUREX exchange has been the catalyst behind the Capital Market Revolution. However, given the ferocity of the revolution, even in its embryonic days on the cusp of the new millennium, it is by no means certain that EUREX will survive the ongoing radical upheaval which ultimately questions the very need for an exchange and the role of the broker – and brings traders into an entirely new dealing marketplace where their skills are often redundant in the face of the demands of new technology.

An "open outcry" process has been the established basis of market transactions since ancient times. Modern stock markets dating from the seventeenth century in London and Amsterdam initially met in coffee houses to discuss trading in conglomerates of sailing ships searching for exciting new import products to be brought from the nascent colonies of their respective empires. Gradually, these meetings became more organized and an exchange structure developed, commoditizing the process of trading in joint stock companies. In the twentieth century, exchanges have become an established way of life, delivering a ready marketplace for shares, bonds, and commodities. Hybrids such as futures, options, and other derivative[1] products have become widely available on exchanges throughout the world.

Thanks to the ingenuity of the human brain, open outcry allows for the facilitation of large trading volumes coupled with a rapid method of discerning a fair value for any commodity.[2] Nevertheless, the actual technology now available to financial markets is largely simple in concept and not ideal for all markets. Yet it is electronic trading that is making vast inroads on the old-established dealing methods. As ever, there are economic factors that have helped render open outcry uncompetitive compared to computerized methodologies.

Open outcry is expensive

> "One has to question whether we need exchanges in their current form. Why maintain a floor for what is essentially an electronic business?"
>
> **Steven M.H. Wallman, Former SEC Commission member**

The truth is that while open outcry is an essentially perfect means of "price discovery", there were inflationary tendencies built into its very make-up. Open outcry also created a cut-throat marketplace with heavy tendencies towards discounting brokerage services. These contrary forces combined literally to tear the open outcry system apart. Once a technological alternative was available, even if not a match for existing methods,

Quite simply, open outcry priced itself out of the market.

there was a stampede to embrace electronic dealing. Quite simply, open outcry priced itself out of the market.

Floor exchanges are staff-intensive. A client speaks to a broker, who rings the floor where a booth clerk takes the order and hand signals or shouts the order into the pit trader, who executes the order prior to handing a trading card to a runner,[3] who takes the order and processes the paperwork. This process is essentially the same on all futures floors. In some larger pits, the broker may require two pit traders, one to show prices to the phone booth staff. Often one person is assigned the job of just commentating on activity in the pit to give clients an insight into market action, while another takes orders directly from clients and from the brokers' offices. Whatever the precise ramifications from one floor to the next, the point is that floor trading is people-intensive and such staff are invariably not cheap to hire. The problem of paying pit traders is further exacerbated by the fact that in such a highly visible environment as pit trading, any dealers (or booth staff) showing anything much beyond a remote semblance of competence are invariably prone to offers of employment from rival firms at higher wages, thanks to the transparency of their talent. This process has resulted in even the most junior staff barely qualified to trade in the pits being sought after in a business where volume has expanded rapidly for the past two decades.

Such escalation in costs would have made little difference to the prospects for open outcry had the cost increases been matched by commensurate revenue growth. Rather, despite the massive explosion in volumes, revenues for brokers have been to all intents and purposes stagnating since the late 1980s. In many ways the floors were victims of their own success. Access to the futures and options exchanges was relatively easy. Anybody sufficiently capitalized could join an exchange and, once through the examination procedures, establish themselves as a broker. This made competition intense in the brokerage business and institutions exploited the competition to reduce their costs.

In the mid-1980s on an exchange such as LIFFE wholesale commissions per contract for a large institution could have been as high as 25 US dollars per round turn. By the late 1990s the same organization would have paid barely 5 dollars. Indeed, discount retail brokers offering no frills to private clients were now offering execution services for 25 dollars – or perhaps even less – to complete novice traders, only trading in a single contract at a time.

While some technological innovations in the back office had helped reduce costs through increased use of computers and decreased paperwork, the costs of being a broker had increased, because of the ever spiraling wage demands of floor traders. Increased volumes meant the companies made profits but margins were under attack. Accountants ever eager to adopt the mantra of cost cutting at the expense of actually improving the capabilities of their banks, as a means to increase profitability, were blinded by headline

> **Increased volumes meant the companies made profits but margins were under attack.**

figures of paying brokerages six-figure checks for services rendered. They were oblivious to the fact that many brokers were now working for little more than a standard transaction fee charged to customers for buying or selling travellers checks. Alas, despite calls from industry magazines such as *Applied Derivatives Trading*, it was too late to save the bean counters from causing the brokers to bleed. The irony was that while cutting brokerage rates by 50 cents per trade really made a big difference to returns for brokers, any traders who need an extra 50 cents off their brokerage to stabilize their trading profitability ought not to be allowed to trade for profit according to even the simplest tenets of risk management.

Crunch time for brokers

"Never before in the history of the financial markets has it been so easy, convenient, and inexpensive for individual investors to participate in the financial markets on their own terms."

Charles Carlson, *The Individual Investor Revolution*

In April 1998, while the mainstream financial news focused on the massive merger mania breaking out in the US banking sector following marriages such as Travellers Corporation with Citibank, the derivatives business was shaken by news from a much smaller bank which nonetheless had a lot of influence in the world of exchange traded derivatives. The Northern Trust Corporation has a retail banking arm barely known outside Chicago. Yet, thanks to geography and a classic example of grasping at opportunity, Northern Trust has a reputation for establishing profitable niche businesses. As *Institutional Investor* commented in December 1997: "Long a fusty, square-shouldered sentinel of old, midwestern money, Northern Trust has been remade over the past decade into a high-tech, high-touch gem of private and institutional trust banking with a steadily growing national reach." Thanks to massive profit growth, it is the only big Chicago bank to remain independent.

Northern Trust has become renowned as an investment manager for super-rich American families. Its reputation as the "Gray Lady of La Salle Street" has long since been shed in its management style, but its imposing façade of Corinthian Columns towering over the corner of La Salle and Monroe streets positively oozes an atmosphere of "old money lives here." Indeed, Northern Trust was originally founded in 1889 by members of the Smith family as a trust bank for Chicago's wealthy. Nowadays Northern Trust has an awesome reputation as an investment manager. When Goldman Sachs partner Robert Rubin quit Wall Street to become Treasury Secretary in the Clinton administration, he placed his nine-figure fortune in the hands of Northern Trust. Apparently Mr Rubin left his money with Northern when he resigned as Treasury Secretary in May 1999 to "spend more time with his family."

The Northern Futures Corporation was a massive player on the Chicago futures exchanges (the Chicago Board of Trade or CBOT and the Chicago Mercantile Exchange or CME). Thanks to a very smart linkage deal negotiated in the early 1980s, Northern had created a joint venture with the leading Anglo-Japanese money-broker Tullett & Tokyo.[4] While all the leading moneybrokers had tried to establish futures exchange brokerage operations, only TNT had survived. Their operations were not hugely profitable but they did serve as an excellent conduit for much higher margin OTC business in other cash and derivatives markets such as FRAs and Swaps. TNT are a huge player in the global futures brokerage business. Through the link-up with TNT, Northern had become one of the largest brokers on both the CBOT and CME.

Alas, in this instance big was no longer beautiful. With margins under pressure, but profitability still intact, Northern no longer had the return on capital it required. Northern wanted out of the futures business and negotiated a deal to transfer Northern staff and the companies' accounts to First Options of Chicago. The Tullett & Tokyo companies created a new strategic alliance with Spear, Leeds & Kellogg, First Options' parent group. Meanwhile,

> The more brokerage rates fall, the less brokers are able to offer a good full-service operation.

Northern strengthened the jewels in the crown of their financial market operations, such as global custody (maintaining share certificates – increasingly in electronic form – for all manners of clients: a bureaucratic process ideally suited to embracing new technology and still a relatively high-margin business).

For those being swept up in the riptides of the Capital Markets Revolution, the core problem remained quite simple: The more brokerage rates fall, the less brokers are able to offer a good full-service operation. The solution increasingly looked like electronic trading.

The electronic alternative

Even in the relatively nascent stages of the personal computer revolution, electronic trading was being touted as an alternative. After abortive developments in Bermuda – amongst others – the first large-scale electronic trading development in derivatives came with GLOBEX. The CME drove the project with software from Reuters, who reputedly spent 100 million US dollars on programing. The whole process was rather a damp squib. Volumes were insignificant compared to daily pit trading. Somewhat embarrassingly for the CME, the GLOBEX system's biggest volume came from the smaller Paris exchange, Marché à Terme International de France (MATIF), whose members largely dominated GLOBEX volume from the moment they joined the system. The CBOT was at one time scheduled to list contracts on GLOBEX but the usual enmity between the Chicago exchanges precluded such co-operation.

However, the vogue for after-hours electronic systems grew rapidly. In Japan the Tokyo International Financial Futures Exchange (TIFFE) opened on screens in 1989. Meanwhile, Europe gradually became a power base for electronic markets. The Frankfurt DTB opened with massive publicity in 1991. MEFF in Spain and OM in Scandinavia both created successful liquid markets for relatively local products in 1991 and 1985 (the latter was the world's first for-profit exchange, a paradigm shift which would become replicated around the world over a decade later). Joining the American-led vogue for after-hours systems, LIFFE produced the Automated Pit Trading (APT) system in 1989. APT was the first system to try to replicate pit trading and proved popular for after-hours trading amongst all tiers of the membership. Nevertheless, until late 1997, although electronic markets had produced some excellent contracts, the serious volumes remained largely in the pits.

Renewed hope for the floor?

"Always remember that technology is far from an opponent to open outcry, rather it is a friend of open outcry."

Daniel Hodson, former CEO, LIFFE

While the bald cost factors favored electronic trading by late 1997, the fact remained that exchange floors could still embrace new technology in an effort to remain competitive. Hand-held order terminals were already available via various companies. Such terminals allowed better audit trail analysis (a key feature to computerized systems), and potentially allowed hard-pressed brokers to trim some staff. There were also potential synergies allowing traders to execute simultaneous orders in cash markets and other exchange or OTC products while standing in a pit. Alas, such technology will likely never reach its ultimate potential before financial markets are largely moved off-floor to a screen-trading environment. Similarly, there were increasing moves towards electronic order routing and back-office systems removing the need for so many booth staff and runners. Electronic devices such as headsets were available in some futures markets to further automate the process. However, as Sydney Futures Exchange (SFE) CEO Les Hosking noted in 1998: "Every investment bank is developing an electronic order-delivery system. Ultimately they are going to say, 'Why the hell do we do it to the edge of the pit and no further?'".

In reality, the floor was not entirely dead, for one very simple reason – computers' incapacity to be flexible. A substantial chunk of business on several markets, particularly the CME and LIFFE, is traded in short-term interest rate contracts (STIRs). With banks seeking to hedge exposure anywhere up to ten years in the future, the number of quarterly contracts on some floors can easily encompass several dozen tradable months. However, while the interest rate on each is important, banks are generally most interested in trading the relative "spreads" between different months or collections of months. By such means mortgage rates can be capped, for instance. The capacity to jump between different contract months on a two-dimensional computer screen remains poor, while the mental agility of specialist floor traders to complete complex mental algorithms to price instantly all manner of related delivery months is still unsurpassed by any computer system.

The innovative dynamic

A big problem for floor trading was that it had become prohibitively expensive to introduce new products. New product launches on derivatives exchanges are a painstaking process. After months, or even years of research, exchange officials solicit commitments from different companies to be respectively market makers or brokers to the new products. The market makers agree to make prices at all times during a trading session while the brokers commit staff to being in the pit throughout the day to transact new business. In return, the designated brokers and market makers receive incentives such as exchange fee "holidays" or rebates during the formative months of a new contract. However, as salaries grew and demand for experienced personnel remained high, institutions were increasingly reluctant to invest the huge amount of staff costs required to deal in new products when the returns might not be seen for several years. Indeed, the LIFFE German Bund futures struggled along for a couple of years with barely significant turnover (compared to the cash market). Then the catalyst of the Berlin Wall falling suddenly propelled the market into an upward spiral which resulted in Bund futures frequently being the biggest contract in the world during 1998 and 1999, challenging the massive CBOT 30-year US Treasury Bond market. Ironically, by the time Bunds were challenging American Treasury futures, volume had already migrated from LIFFE to the electronic DTB.

> Introducing a new contract on computer screens is much simpler and cheaper for all parties.

Nowadays, the innovative dynamic favors electronic markets. Introducing a new contract on computer screens is much simpler and cheaper for all parties. Market makers can make a price in several markets from an office environment, while brokers can access markets directly from their terminals without requiring extra staff to process orders.

In an industry that has thrived on new product innovation during recent years and with the threat of economic and monetary union (EMU) reducing the number of available contracts in Europe (and thus the thriving business of intermarket spread trading), many brokers – not just in Europe but throughout the world – are eagerly awaiting new products.

What threatened LIFFE?

The LIFFE U-turn was unparalleled in capital markets history. The exchange changed just about every facet of its organization and operation in a matter of months. The motivation was the inroads made into the London market's volumes by the electronic DTB operated out of Frankfurt.

The primary battleground between DTB and LIFFE was in German ten-year Government Bonds (Bunds). For years LIFFE had dominated the market. By March 1997 the DTB had only managed to capture a very paltry share of 35 percent of Bund futures trading. In April this creaked up to 37.5 percent, but after six years of head-to-head contest progress was hardly significant. Then as 1997 progressed, volume began to drift upwards on the DTB. It was not a passive situation: the Frankfurt management had gone on a no-holds-barred attempt to coax the business away from the London market. Turnover reached 43 percent in July 1997 when trading hours were extended by 90 minutes. Conveniently this matched the opening hours of the LIFFE contracts, although DTB officials claimed the move was purely to make the market more accessible to American users.

By September 1997 the gloves were off and the knuckle-dusters on, in the fight for market share in Bund and Bobl contracts (futures and options). Exchange or clearing fees for trading were waived at both the DTB and LIFFE. As Steve Black commented in *ADT*: "Other than calling in the stealth bombers – let's hope it's not raining – they must be running out of tactics by now, surely? Perhaps they'll start trying to outbid one another on how much they'll pay us to trade on their particular exchange. Sounds good to me. "

On 4 September the Deutsche Börse (the stockmarket parent of DTB) upped the stakes further by announcing that they would operate as a common market with the Swiss Options and Financial Futures Exchange (SOFFEX) under the EUREX banner.

By October, LIFFE's share of the Bund business was down to 52 percent. However, the DTB's policy of disseminating its screens far and wide (by now it had members operating direct to Frankfurt from a network including London, Paris, Chicago, and New York), often on very advantageous terms, was making a serious impact. The ten US DTB members alone were contributing some 18 percent of Bund volume. It was a technological warning that LIFFE failed to heed until it was too late for their Bund business. The London exchange appeared to be paying too much attention to its newly secured status of second biggest exchange in the world.

> The London exchange appeared to be paying too much attention to its new status of second biggest exchange in the world.

The full frontal assault on LIFFE's Bund business went ballistic on 1 January 1998. The DTB dropped up-front admission and annual membership fees for full members and market makers and slashed those for clearing members. Telecommunication line fees were also dropped, replaced by a minimum transaction fee of DEM 4500 per month.

On 22 October 1997 a turning point had been reached. The DTB surpassed LIFFE's Bund market share with 52 percent of that day's volume. From then on, the Germans never looked back.

LIFFE feels the heat

Within weeks of its spectacular 15th anniversary celebrations, it seemed as if LIFFE had finally blinked when looking into the headlights of the DTB juggernaut threatening the core Bund business. The LIFFE Board announced a "strategic away day" for 8 July. It largely reaffirmed LIFFE's faith in the status quo, even when its business was threatening to crumble away in front of its eyes. Open outcry would continue and the expensive property developments at Spitalfields (a whole new floor) and on the old Stock Exchange floor (an overflow facility for LIFFE's stretched existing pit capacity) were still going ahead. It looked like LIFFE had lost the plot in the face of a very determined opponent.

After a few months of relative silence, big-league exchange politicking broke out with a vengeance during March 1998. First up was LIFFE, which had hesitated in the screen versus floor poker game. The London exchange opted to develop a world-beating screen-based system in an attempt to wrestle back Bund volume from Frankfurt's (or rather "virtual" Frankfurt's) DTB exchange.

LIFFE loses its nerve

Suddenly LIFFE was also attempting to rebalance the economics of brokerage operations – which it would not even recognize as a problem a mere six months earlier. The previous July's away day jolly had done little to assuage the growing concerns amongst many LIFFE members and users. On 9 March the exchange unexpectedly announced the results of a more comprehensive "strategic review" which would be put to members at an EGM on 12 May. The depth and scope of the change evidenced an organization that was beginning to reconsider every aspect of its ethos:

> The exchange will develop, by Q4 of 1999, a world leading automated trading system to enable the intraday listing of all major contracts, notwithstanding that such products will also continue to be made available on the floor.

> Proposals should be adopted which will have the effect of maximising the commercial attractiveness and effectiveness of access to the new trading system – which the Board expects will include a different relationship between Exchange share ownership and trading rights.

> The Board recognises that these are likely to lead to a revision of the corporate structure of the market and will publish recommendations – including products to be listed on the new system – on 17 April and submit them to an EGM of the market on 12 May.

> Transaction fees will be cut from 1 April, to be funded by a reduction in budgeted expenditure of GBP 30–40 million.

> Investment in the efficiency of open outcry trading and the renewal of core systems will continue. The Board will review the premises requirements.

> There will be a review of the rules, procedures, and other activities and processes of the Exchange with the object of maximising the flow of international wholesale market business to the Exchange.

The apparent shift in emphasis towards screen trading naturally caused annoyance amongst the locals. To some it came as no great surprise but to many it looked like a vile plot to put them out of business. The vested interests of exchanges are frequently the market's worst enemies.

There was much consternation at the time. Given the extent of the bombshell to hit the membership, this was hardly surprising.

The vested interests of exchanges are frequently the market's worst enemies.

For a start, many members wondered why there had to be a wait of almost 18 months before the new trading system could be introduced. Admittedly, if it did handle STIR contracts effectively in the spreading department then the floor would be deserted within days. Equally, some members wondered why the existing after-hours APT system could not be used by all contracts in the interim. As APT was the closest thing to replicating pit trading on a computer terminal the first-generation screen-trading systems had ever managed, there was some justification in this query. The worrying factor on everybody's minds was that by the last quarter of 1999 it could be too late to save any of LIFFE's business.

EUREX comes up trumps?

On 18 March the CBOT and EUREX announced a "letter of intent" to form a far-reaching alliance. It was intended as being no less than "the basis for a global derivatives market" as it was intended the plan "eventually will be rounded out with a strategic partner from the Asia-Pacific region."

The news, announced at the exclusive Boca Raton Resort during the FIA's annual conference, stunned many of the 2000 delegates from all over the world. After making little impact on even the domestic derivatives environment for a decade, the German-led

EUREX alliance was suddenly in bed with the leading global market. For LIFFE, the effect was even more marked, as only months earlier the London exchange had suspended its joint open outcry linkage for German Bunds and US Treasury Bonds on each other's exchanges. At the time, it had looked as if the CBOT was merely seeking to expand its after-hours "Project A" system. Now, it transpired, it was actually looking at a radical deal which appeared to put LIFFE on the backburner and EUREX in pole position in the run-up to EMU. The fact that the CBOT and EUREX were confident that their global communications network would be operational by Q4 of 1998, a full year ahead of LIFFE's radical new Automated Trading Platform (ATP would therefore replace APT), was a further irritant for LIFFE. That the CBOT and EUREX would have dual market access from a single screen (for daytime EUREX and after-hours CBOT Project A) by Q2 1999, only rubbed salt into LIFFE's wounds.

> The big problem was that LIFFE had delayed any discussion, let alone a move, to electronic trading for at least a year too long.

The immediate reaction was that the entire affair boded ill for LIFFE. However, while it appeared bleak on the surface, there were some possible straws for LIFFE to clutch at. The big problem was that LIFFE had delayed any discussion, let alone a move, to electronic trading for at least a year too long. Ironically, there were many heavy investors on the board buying new technology for their brokerages (often on DTB) while keeping LIFFE on the open outcry track. Meanwhile, despite reigning supreme in the Bunds, the DTB had made nothing more than a minuscule dent in the LIFFE Euromark volumes. In the key three-month Euromarks, the DTB system still could not cope with the intricacies of simultaneously pricing back months, spreads, and more complex strategies – unlike the then current versions of *Homo sapiens* who traded them all day long on the LIFFE floor. Regardless of geographical penetration, the DTB system still could not beat open outcry for outright price discovery.

Meanwhile, the impending arrival of the Euro currency between 1999 and 2002 was clouding the horizon. Finally, there was the fact that, having promised much, almost all derivatives exchange linkages to-date had achieved little and had ultimately been dissolved, often amidst some rancor. For every good, successful link-up, the ante-rooms and plush hotel suites of international financial conference venues were scattered with the wreckage of numerous failed agreements. The CME/SIMEX Eurodollar Mutual Offset (MOS) link in the 1980s was a rare gem. It launched the Singapore market on to the forefront of the world stage and secured vast swathes of business for the CME in Asia.

Equally, electronic trading platform agreements had been almost universally unsuccessful to date. The Reuters-developed GLOBEX had been inconspicuosuly unsuccesful until the French MATIF joined it, and even then it failed to truly reach its potential. "If GLOBEX was a dog then Project A was a dog with fleas," to paraphrase Gordon Gecko. The fact remained that the members of the CBOT were not interested in trading Bund contracts on their beloved floor (any more than they were interested in trading their own contracts on their Project A system), which made it difficult to see them finding EUREX products more attractive once they were on the screens encompassed by the alliance. The fact remained that Middle America was not overly fussed about what happened in the rest of the world. Chicago had built its reputation on Midwestern grains and other commodities. Its successful financial products had all contained a US dollar component.

Schadenfreude makes its mark

On 23 March 1998 the Deutsche Börse (DTB's parent company) took out full-page "open letter to LIFFE" advertisements in the *Financial Times*, *The Times*, and *Wall Street Journal*, offering to implement the DTB system at LIFFE – for free. "Why don't we work together and strengthen the new pan-European trading grid?" it asked. LIFFE promptly issued a testy reply, pointing out that not only did the DTB system have several deficiencies, but following intensive evaluation of all available electronic systems – it did not score as highly as several alternatives!

Ironically, the largest and most irritating flaw in the exchanges' increasing tendency to try and points-score off one another was the fact that both markets were still too remote from their end users in terms of finding out what they actually wanted. The big players in the financial business are big, very big. In fact they are huge. Each and every one of the world's major exchanges was being "supported" by a monstrous bureaucracy which appeared to be getting ever larger – although many traders could not see any difference in the ultimate service to the end user. As exchange bureaucracies were spiralling out of control, there was a great danger of complacency overwhelming the premier exchanges.

Technology can undoubtedly facilitate more flexible exchanges. The SFE quoted this as one of the reasons for wanting to switch to computerized trading. It could also permit new entrants to the exchange

> Exchanges need to spend their time interfacing with traders and actually trying to improve the dealer's lot.

business. The Swedish OM organization is a good example of a niche exchange, operating on a "for profit" basis and, therefore, largely bereft of the vast overheads and bureaucracy so beloved by its weightier brethren. In the foreign exchange market, the Reuters 2000–2 dealing system wreaked havoc with the profitability of this sector of the money-broking industry in no time at all.

Exchanges need to spend their time interfacing with traders and actually trying to improve the dealer's lot. The current, endless power conferencing around the world portrays an image of an industry that is increasingly out of touch with its clients. There is a third way to create mega exchanges – and the sooner the existing players realize it, the better it will be for them.

A matter of LIFFE and death

As we discussed in the Prologue, the fall from grace of LIFFE CEO Daniel Hodson was swift and merciless. In the most aggressive portals of capitalism it was always thus. Nevertheless, it would be unfair to point all the blame, or even a significant quantity, directly at the LIFFE CEO's door. Certainly Hodson made errors, but he also fell victim to some significant lack of foresight by his exchange Board. The errors were those that many mortals could have missed and indeed Chairman Jack Wigglesworth and CEO Hodson both failed to see coming. Or did they? Shortly after standing down as Chairman, Jack Wigglesworth noted that "Our members would not even let us talk about electronic trading for the last two years."[5] This was a remarkable statement, as other Board members laid the blame for not discussing open outcry squarely at Wigglesworth's door.

The LIFFE Board had had several discontented members for some months. Indeed, in the global business of derivatives trading the LIFFE Board found itself becoming somewhat of a political football. The Board is elected by the members and each corporation has one vote. Exchange boards often are over-representative of brokers compared to traders, as the former are not only more actively involved in all aspects of the derivatives business (many institutional traders have a relatively narrow focus) but equally brokers, by their very *raison d'être* of selling services to lots of traders, tend to be better known.

The problem then arose that some LIFFE directors appeared to be maintaining faith in LIFFE's espousal of open outcry, providing "steady as she goes" encouragement at Board meetings. Yet at the same time, there was significant evidence of these self-same board members actually joining the DTB and buying in electronic trading capacity for their companies simultaneously. Board acrimony reached a peak on 26 March when LIFFE announced details of exchange fee reductions. By all accounts, the decision process was far from smooth. Reportedly, up to 40 percent of the Board stormed out before the end of the meeting. Talk of resignations abounded. LIFFE looked on the verge of tearing itself apart. Something had to give.

The meaning of LIFFE?

In a blizzard of announcements in the wake of the acrimonious Board meeting, LIFFE adopted a new management structure. The exchange moved from being a mutual organization owned by membership without a profit motive, to being a fully for-profit corporation permitting third party (i.e. non-market) shareholders, and revised trading rights.

In July the Board announced the first full-time salaried Executive Chairman (previous appointees had been elected Board members, and representatives of member firms) on a three-year term. The appointee was Brian Williamson CBE. The City of London cheered. At 53, Williamson was already a legendary figure in financial markets. One of the original directors, a driving force behind the establishment of LIFFE (and Chairman from 1985 to 1988), Williamson retained icon status amongst the LIFFE community. Of his few detractors, one retiring LIFFE Board member referred to him as "a bloody control freak". "It's about time LIFFE had one!" was the retort of another senior City figure. As a founder (along with Mark Davies and Christopher Sharples) of Gerard and National Intercommodities, a leading global brokerage, Williamson was sufficiently wealthy not to require the Executive Chairman's salary. For Williamson, it was a case of returning to LIFFE to bring it into the new millennium from a position of renewed strength. It was a challenge he would relish.

On Tuesday 21 July 1998, Daniel Hodson resigned as LIFFE CEO. Hodson stated that Brian Williamson:

> is exactly the right person for the task ahead and, in common with the entire LIFFE community, I wish him great success. We have together concluded that it is absolutely essential that he has a clear run at the enormous challenges facing the Exchange. To this end, and in accordance with my own aspirations, the Chairman has agreed that I may now step down as Chief Executive ... For myself, I have always maintained that if you stay more than five years in a job, you're potentially in extra time, particularly in a highly demanding, change oriented one like this – and I've done five and a half. Clearly the job is unfinished. But it is time for new

leadership with fresh vision and rekindled energy to take this marvellous institution towards the world leadership to which it justly aspires.

Williamson returned to the reins at LIFFE determined to shape the market to his new vision. It was a vision to which only Williamson was privy but it was soon clear that radical surgery was required for LIFFE to meet his new model. Hodson had already left the field clear for him almost two weeks before Williamson officially assumed office on 3 August.

Meanwhile, even after the difficult period culminating in his resignation, Daniel Hodson retained his usual self-effacing charm. Prior to a spot of gardening at his English country house, Hodson departed for his Greek holiday villa after placing the following note in *The Times* diary column: "To hire: energetic and experienced chief executive with a proven thick skin and a sense of humour. Will travel."

In a matter of months, LIFFE had been left reeling from loss of market share and ultimately internal dissension.

At the August Board meeting, long-time director David Kyte arrived at the meeting armed with a PATS trading screen on a laptop. When he had given a live demonstration of trading on to the DTB using the PATS terminal, Kyte announced: "This is the future of trading, I hereby resign." Given that long-time local and clearing firm owner Kyte had in fact been one of the most vocal opponents to even the vaguest board discussion of electronic trading two years earlier, it was a remarkable turnaround.

In a matter of months, LIFFE had been left reeling from loss of market share and ultimately internal dissension. In fact, the process of adjusting to the Capital Market Revolution was barely begun. However, there were promising signs that at last the market had got on top of the various problems facing it immediately and in the near future.

The LIFFE revolution

Anything which anybody within LIFFE had ever held sacred now came under direct fire. In a whirlwind process, Williamson set about not so much reshaping the exchange as entirely demolishing everything and starting again.

Williamson wasted no time in making clear his intention to get his "hands dirty."

> The Exchange's customers are my number one priority and I will be embarking on an extensive consultation programme with them as soon as my appointment begins. But I want them to know that I am resolved to act with speed and determination.

> The Exchange must continue to play a full part in maintaining and growing international business in the City of London to ensure that it remains the pre-eminent international financial centre.

The last bombshell of a hectic 1998, LIFFE reserved for November, when the exchange announced that it was: "To take decisive action to restructure its business to meet the needs of its customers in the future. It will make access to the exchange cheaper and easier for users and achieve efficiencies by internal restructuring and cost-cutting."

With South African Hugh Freedburg now employed as CEO, LIFFE was finally ready to put the nails into the coffin of the *ancien régime*. As Williamson put it:

> We have to deliver an efficient trading platform together with the products that our customers want, at a price they are prepared to pay. It is clear that nothing remotely like our current cost base is sustainable and that we shall have to cut jobs to remain competitive. We will also achieve cost savings by overhauling our regulatory structure so that it suits today's market. In addition, there is the potential for us to win new business by forging new links with other business partners, in London and internationally.

These new links could include network and technology providers, exchanges, clearing houses and related businesses. Williamson had already appointed a council of wise men – leading City of London figures – to advise the exchange on its future strategy.

Freedburg was no less forthright: "We will be driven by the marketplace and our focus must be on meeting the needs of customers. Customers expect efficiency, ease of access, flexibility and speed. We will deliver the right technology and the right products at the right price." At last a leading exchange had actually grasped the nettle and was seeking to adopt a new model environment with which to secure the continuation of the exchange. ADT's Exchange commentator Steve Black was more forthright:

> **Customers expect efficiency, ease of access, flexibility and speed.**

> It's a great theme – in fact, unless certain other exchanges change their attitudes, it could be a world beater. Just so long, of course, as LIFFE haven't left it too late … We don't normally harp back to the past, but the people who are responsible for not appointing this pair some 12–18 months earlier should all be taken out and shot.

The view from America

The year 1998 marked the 150th anniversary of the CBOT. On 18 February 1997 the venerable exchange had moved to a new home. Chicago Mayor Richard Daley inaugurated the largest trading floor in the world, occupying some 60 000 square feet at a cost of 182 million US dollars. As the Chairman, Pat Arbor, looked out upon the floor during early 1998, he had no idea that the next 12 months would be so tumultuous for either him or the world's oldest and largest futures exchange. There had been trading on the CBOT in agricultural products since the last widespread mainland European food blight. As Lafayette witnessed the last of three French revolutions in his remarkable lifetime, the CBOT was already trading cash grains. Forward trading had begun on 13 March 1851, while 3000 bushels of corn for June delivery marked the first futures transaction as long ago as 1865.

Arbor, even during the first six months of 1998, had endured a bumpy ride. In March members vetoed a proposal to raise Arbor's salary from 240 000 to 400 000 dollars per annum. Ironically, even if it had been agreed, this raise would still have left the CBOT Chairman trailing the best local trader incomes by many millions per annum.

At the CBOT the LIFFE open outcry link had been gently discarded. The groundbreaking alliance with EUREX shook the derivatives firmament. Nevertheless, the volumes piled up and the CBOT remained top dog. Even merger talks with longstanding Chicago rival the CME, were ongoing. However, first up was the common clearing issue.

With OTC business, where there is no common clearing, institutions must deal with each other using credit lines – a series of credit relationships where different-sized banks all have different quantities of "lines" (ability to deal) related to their creditworthiness. While the system tends to work well overall, the danger remains of a counter-party default causing a bank to lose a profitable position.

Therefore a clearing house has several advantages. For one, it permits institutions and individuals to meet and transact business on an exchange without having to be concerned about the other parties' creditworthiness. Equally, even when the likes of Drexel Burnham Lambert collapsed in the 1980s, independent local traders and institutions alike were not blighted by losses suffered from dealing with the ill-fated kings of junk bonds.

The problem in Chicago was that the two big exchanges, the CBOT and the CME, both operated separate clearing houses. This was bureaucratically and fiscally cumbersome for members of both markets. With the CME having the biggest short interest rate contract in the world (the three-month Eurodollar deposits) and the CBOT holding the Treasury Note and Bond complex on its floor, there was also the fact that trading spreads between these and other contracts across different markets became relatively expensive for traders interested in both markets. Margins tended to be offset to some degree by certain combinations of trades. In the case of traders wishing to trade the American yield curve, they had to pay margins to both markets. The same applied if spreading commodities listed on the two different exchanges. This inefficiency was not something that could be tolerated in the new financial climate. The Chicago exchanges needed to merge their clearing quickly in order to be seen to be reforming their history of enmity between the neighboring markets.

Despite strong CBOT volume in the first half of 1998, Arbor's fate would be surprisingly sealed in the second half of 1998.

The burdens of individual membership

"The two Chicago exchanges are on a path towards mutually assured self-destruction, and it's working."

Verne Sedlacek, COO, John Henry and Company

In the USA, as opposed to more corporatized Europe, membership of exchanges tends to be organized on an individual level. While this means a greater degree of democracy insofar as every single pit trader (including hundreds of independent "locals") can each vote, it can also hamper an exchange's attempts to progress. The Chicago exchanges have suffered when members have put their (short-term) self-interest ahead of the needs of the market.

In early September 1998 this militancy on the part of the membership resulted in a petition to the CBOT Board complaining about the terms of the deal to create common clearing. At a stormy Board meeting, the CBOT Board "voted to rescind its support for creating a common clearing house with the CME." This was despite the CME apparently agreeing to a last-minute request by the CBOT that their clearing house be used as the corporate structure for the joint entity.

> The Chicago exchanges have suffered when members have put their (short-term) self-interest ahead of the needs of the market.

CME Chairman Scott Gordon immediately expressed "disappointment and frustration" at the CBOT's withdrawal. FIA Chairman, Ronald M. Hersch was equally upset:

We are extremely disappointed by the CBOT's retreat from their commitment and the failure of the two Chicago exchanges to come together on a customer-driven initiative. It is obvious that exchange politics continue to prevent these institutions from supporting the type of cost-driven initiatives needed to grow our markets.

At the Burgenstock conference only days later, the FIA's President John Damgard was little short of incandescent. Damgard, a tall and somewhat dashing figure, a classic example of the laconic but sharp Midwestern American, could barely contain his anger: "It's a very sad day in Chicago," he noted, bristling with indignation.

The Burgenstock meeting itself was somewhat of a curious affair. The leading European conference for derivatives markets was marked by a large amount of jostling for position and claiming of territory without any particular announcements of note. Nevertheless, the stress was showing for many leading exchange executives.

A press conference, called by the CBOT and EUREX to announce the cementing of their co-operation agreement after the lawyers and regulators had had their say, left many onlookers wondering quite what the CBOT had let itself in for. The event itself was a sort of corporate love-in and it only served to underline concerns amongst many industry onlookers that the dynamics of the derivatives industry were beginning to pass the grandees of the CBOT by. They looked increasingly out of place when sitting alongside the smooth technocrats of EUREX led by Jorg Franke. When CBOT CEO Tom Donovan stated categorically that "EUREX has the best electronic system in the world … it doesn't go down," many onlookers had to stifle a laugh. Whether Donovan had merely suffered a momentary lapse on account of jet lag or the Alpine air in the Swiss resort, his comment was never adequately explained. Quite simply there was no serious basis in fact for such a statement. There was much documentary evidence of the DTB's system continually slowing down in mid-session and leaving orders within the system, much to the horror of traders who were powerless to amend their orders.

Indeed, the entire EUREX apparatus was looking increasingly

shaky. (In a delicious sideswipe at the EUREX platform, MATIF Chairman Jean-François Théodore noted later in the Burgenstock conference: "You can claim you are a benchmark but that does not make you a benchmark, even when you are old."). With the platform ageing rapidly, the system's massive growth was now causing it considerable problems. The CBOT management appeared oblivious to this at Burgenstock. It looked dangerously as if the CBOT may have married EUREX in haste and would end up repenting at leisure.

Meanwhile, LIFFE had held a meet-and-greet cocktail party with its new executive Chairman, Brian Williamson who, unlike his equivalents from other markets, spared the assembled multitude any comments about his grand designs for the future. Sipping his whisky and oozing charisma, Williamson nevertheless proved the most enigmatic draw of the conference.

Pat Arbor had, like Tom Donovan, looked out of his depth at the Burgenstock meeting. This was a remarkable turnaround for Arbor who had a deserved reputation as a survivor both in trading and trading politics. A sleek bald figure with a reputation as somewhat of a Lothario, Arbor had long been a smooth operator but nonetheless a somewhat colorful figure in the Chicago trading community. Arbor famously lost a paternity suit in the 1970s to a famous *Playboy* centerfold.

The very act of inking the deal with EUREX did Arbor immeasurable damage in the eyes of the membership. In a vote on 9 December 1998, Arbor was unexpectedly voted out by members increasingly vexed at the prospect of open outcry being usurped by what was seen as Arbor's advocacy of screen trading. Members were uncertain what if anything was likely to benefit them from the EUREX–CBOT deal. The CBOT had already spent several million dollars on the deal and yet members could see no tangible value, aside from conspicuous quantities of glossy direct mail assuring them this was a move for the future benefit of the market. The consultants may have been handsomely rewarded, but the membership of the market was on the verge of revolt. Meanwhile, a vast number of pit traders did not want the existing food chain involving the floor threatened, regardless of the fundamental merits of any exchange technology/linkage deal. A relative unknown beyond the walls of the CBOT, local trader David Brennan was elected Chairman in a move that startled the world's markets. Already the first reaction to the revolution was under way.

Notes

1 Derivatives are so called as they are products "derived" from cash markets.

2 The process of discerning a fair value for a market is known as "price discovery." By its very nature of having a large "crowd" *in situ* to make a market, open outcry is an excellent method of "price discovery." Where a market facilitates trading easily (leading to strong volume) this is referred to as "liquidity" and is again a major benefit to open outcry methods.

3 Some exchange floors, such as the grains room at the Chicago Board of Trade (CBOT) are so large that another staff member "a runner" must actually run with the order down from the phone booths to the side of the pit.

4 Moneybrokers traditionally had their basis in the foreign exchange market and deal with large institutions and banks exclusively. Their business is huge but largely takes place directly between counterparties via a broker without recourse to an exchange (known as "over the counter" or "OTC" business).

5 Jack Wigglesworth, *Institutional Investor*, June 1998.

CHAPTER 2

The New Reality

Changing the food chain for ever

> "For future historians, the salient fact of twentieth-century finance will be the sharp erosion of banker power – that is, the dwindling role of the financial inter-mediary. Bankers are glorified go-betweens, conduits for capital flows. During the twentieth century ... the banker's intermediary role in the financial equation has declined. A horrid term is sometimes employed to describe this phenomenon – disintermediation."
>
> **Ron Chernow, *The Death of the Banker*, Pimlico Books, 1997**

If the only danger posed to exchanges was that their historic open outcry dealing mechanisms were being superseded by computers, then many exchange personnel would sleep easier at night. Rather, there is a dreaded "D" word that has kept every senior exchange official awake at night at some point during the past few years. Those who deny it are either lying or so severely out of touch as to be prime unemployment fodder within the near future. The word in question is "disintermediation" – the process of removing middle-men from transactions.

Disintermediation threatens the firmament of every single existing marketplace, not to mention all the other middlemen (in each and every walk of commercial life). Disintermediation is no respecter of ages, or history, or values. It is simply a bald economic fact of life. If an exchange or a broker, or any other type of intermediary cannot justify their part in the process of adding value to a transaction, then their place in the food chain will be skipped through. This is the New

Reality. As Steve Black succinctly surmised in *ADT*: "No one person or party's place in the trading chain is now assured." The size of any broker, counterparty or exchange before they are struck by the revolutionary fervor is irrelevant. Indeed the larger the organization and the more power it has traditionally wielded in recent times, the swifter and more dramatic will be its downfall.

In the previous chapter we looked at the CBOT, the biggest derivatives exchange in the world. Throughout the 1980s and 1990s volumes soared and there seemed to be few – if any – problems with open outcry. On the surface, this was irrefutably correct. However, overheads coupled with a squeeze by institutions on brokerage levels have led to open outcry essentially shooting itself in the foot, despite screen-based alternatives still largely failing to mimic sufficiently the flexibility of face-to-face dealing techniques. Indeed, it is a mixture of the cost accountants' ongoing desire to squeeze brokerage rates and the crowd of pit traders largely pricing themselves out of the market that has undermined open outcry, rather than any particularly stunning technological innovations. Nevertheless, the information revolution itself has major implications for financial markets, which we will address presently.

With open outcry apparently so successful, the CBOT has remained somewhat fixated with what looks suspiciously like a lose–lose situation for the senior management. If it embraces new technology and goes screen trading, then the floor membership will be in uproar. If the CBOT fails to take account of the "New Reality," then the fateful "D" word could quite easily see the CBOT wiped out within a handful of years. The election as Chairman of reactionary Michael Brennan, when his predecessor suggested tactical alliance with the EUREX screen-based exchange, shows that there are many battles yet to be fought before all counterparties to open outcry understand the problems which lie ahead of them.

Indeed, the CBOT's new Chairman, David Brennan, increasingly appeared to be grasping at straws even before he had spent 6 months in office. On a fact finding mission to Europe, press cynics noted that the only "fact" Brennan had learnt was what an API (the open architecture protocol) was although his description of this nugget of information to a subsequent press conference appeared muddled. A fumbling attempt to replace CBOT CEO Tom Donovan (himself looking increasingly out of his depth in the New Reality) failed and Brennan had to make a humiliating and unprecedented public apology to the board of directors. Then finally, Brennan, the Chairman elected to get rid of the EUREX deal, announced in early May 1999 that the CBOT would in fact attempt to resurrect the deal with the Europeans after a secret weekend meeting in Monte Rotondo, Italy. Chairman Brennan commented, "The time is now right for a business alliance with EUREX and it has my complete support." Many onlookers were confused as to why suddenly the deal looked so good when Brennan had campaigned for the Chairmanship expressly to scupper this deal. Meanwhile, the CBOT CEO Tom Donovan remarked, "This EUREX alliance will allow us to meet and beat all competition." It was doubtless not lost on the competition that the CBOT had already seen their number one spot taken by the EUREX market. The CBOT continued to look like a market bereft of inspiration and one which could, even with a EUREX co-operation deal in place, yet prove to be the biggest casualty of the Capital Market Revolution.

Until the DTB/EUREX took the dominant position in volume in German Bund contracts, one law had remained faithful in derivatives markets. The exchange that got volume into a contract first won the day. It was true when the Americans launched their Treasury Bond and Eurodollar contracts at the CBOT and CME respectively. It was true when LIFFE launched a host of European contracts based around Italian Bonds and German interest rates. The Barcelona-based MEFF (electronic) exchange had a stranglehold on Spanish Government Bonds which LIFFE could barely dent when it experimented with its own Bonos contract.

Then the Frankfurt-based exchange, with an immense array of incentives and enticements, not to mention a hefty marketing budget, finally wrested control of the German Bund business away from LIFFE after almost a decade of trying. However, the fact that one exchange had poached a top international contract from another was not an isolated incidence. Indeed, in the future, exchanges will find it increasingly difficult to hold contracts on their exchange.

The New Reality dictates that all exchanges are now in a position to compete with each other. More significantly, the cost of entering the exchange provision market has now become a great deal cheaper. At the time of writing, the only thing halting a global free-for-all in financial markets is the regulation. Equally, however, it is the very regulation of financial markets that is ultimately driving many facets of the disintermediation process in the first place.

> **The New Reality dictates that all exchanges are now in a position to compete with each other.**

New market solutions

> "The status quo won't do."
>
> **John Damgard, President, FIA**

John Damgard is absolutely right. The status quo won't do. Exchanges must adapt if they are to have a hope of survival. Since before the dawn of the last millennium, financial markets have been localized operations pivoting around face-to-face dealing centered on exchange market floors. Indeed, such markets have been largely unchanged since the ancient world. In the modern age the CBOT celebrated its 150th anniversary in 1998 with a mode of dealing essentially identical to that with which it began operations during continental Europe's last widespread food blight.

With the rise of the Internet all aspects of financial markets, and with it the way many areas of broader business operate, are threatened by the Capital Market Revolution. From the humblest retail stock market punter through to vast interbank dealing operations, the future is radically different. The development of e-markets is a dynamic environment showing every sign of accelerating as new media trading opportunities explode.

Cantor Fitzgerald was initially unsuccessful with its attempts to wrest business from the CBOT with its own Cantor Fitzgerald Financial Futures Exchange. However, with the capacity to become fully automated and provide cash bond and futures dealing all within one screen, it was too early to write off the US's first electronic futures market. Meanwhile, a series of former senior New York and Chicago exchange officials, backed by leading online stockbroker E-Trade, have created the International Securities Exchange (ISE) a direct competitor to the Chicago Board Options Exchange (CBOE), a market specializing in US equity options. Ironically, demonstrating just how much many aspects of market are being driven by European innovation, the ISE is using European technology for its market. It is technology developed by OM systems – a Swedish firm which despite the high taxes and paternalistic socialism of that Scandinavian country has become a leading technology supplier at the forefront of capitalist activity.

The fact is that these days if you wish to open up an exchange, you can simply call into one of OM's offices in the world and look at creating an exchange using bespoke software which can be amended to fit your needs in a matter of weeks. When Patrick Young ran out of time on a visit to OM's London office, he was able to walk into their Sydney CBD offices and run through the identical ORC trading software a few days later. Today the whole ethos of a financial district being central to a marketplace is comprehensively undermined. Direct access to the world's exchanges will soon be available at the click of a mouse button through dedicated lines to any market in the world from any market in the world. If you want it now, you can get direct access through the Internet without having to wait for the installation of dedicated telephone lines.[1]

> Today the whole ethos of a financial district being central to a marketplace is comprehensively undermined.

New markets, new capital

> "Locals can and are beginning to use electronic systems effectively."
>
> **Roz Wilton, MD Transaction Products, Reuters PLC.**

One key argument for capital market Luddites is that the revolution is simply doomed to fail on account of a lack of liquidity. Throughout history the core ease of dealing, "liquidity" of financial markets, has largely been provided by varying forms of independent capital. On the New York Stock Exchange (NYSE) specialists were typically family-run businesses, although many equity markets have increasingly benefited from corporate capital providing liquidity in more recent years as the equity bull market developed. On the derivatives markets throughout the world the markets are reliant on the independent "local" traders to provide liquidity to facilitate smooth transactions between large institutions.

The business as the locals have been used to transacting it is doomed. Nevertheless, that won't stop those who see a very lucrative livelihood being threatened behaving like the Luddites of the early nineteenth century who sought to destroy the looms and the factories which they felt threatened their livelihood. Ironically, it was the Industrial Revolution that propelled the earnings of the average worker to highs previously undreamed of during the previous millennia.

There is massive new opportunity for independent capital within the New Reality."

Many people have long held the viewpoint that private independent liquidity provision will be muscled out by corporate capital provision. The Catalyst Institute, a US think-tank on financial markets, issued a report in 1994 by Washington University Assistant Professor, S. Craig Pirrong, entitled "Derivatives, Exchanges, Liquidity and Locals, A Look To The Future". In it, Dr Pirrong noted: "Small local traders are relatively unimportant suppliers of liquidity on automated exchanges which reflects the structure of the costs incurred to participate in a computerized trading system."

Ironically, the passage of time has been cruel to Dr Pirrong's linear analyses. The sheer dynamism of the information age has created a whole new industry of companies providing computer solutions for online traders via the Internet and direct access to exchanges and new market mechanisms. There is now a veritable army of new micro providers of information solutions to enable traders in all shapes and sizes of institutions to trade direct to all forms of global markets. Meanwhile, individuals are already embracing such direct information solutions to permit them to deal online. In the New Reality the old-style locals are dead. However, the New Reality provides extensive new opportunities for a whole new breed of diversified independent traders for whom access to dealing in New York equities or Tokyo derivatives is increasingly simple, regardless of whether they are in Amman, Beirut, Belfast, Harare, Jakarta, San Francisco, or Tangier.

There is massive new opportunity for independent capital within the New Reality.

Survival of the fittest

"I can't understand why people are frightened by new ideas. I'm frightened by old ones."

John Cage

Many traders have already adapted to the wonders of electronic trading. The new maxim for the e-local is "be anywhere, do anything, at anytime." The lifestyle and opportunities for an e-local are examined in Chapter 6.

Nevertheless, there are those who do not want the relatively solitary trading experience. Having enjoyed the camaraderie of the floor, they seek out opportunities to trade in some form of dealing community. In response to this demand, there are increasing numbers of dealing rooms where freelance traders can rent a desk space. Such "trading arcades" have existed in some format or another for a century. Wall Street histories of the Roaring Twenties positively burgeon with anecdotes of people watching the ticker tape pass on price information. Nowadays the "trading arcade", like its amusement arcade cousin, is a much more high-tech version of the original idea. In London in 1998, a leading LIFFE clearing agent of locals,[2] Kyte Futures, founded a Trading Arcade on London's Cannon Street with some 60 terminals provided by the PATS company run by Thomas Theys which all offered live access to the EUREX market. Rather than having to write down orders and hand them across a counter to a broker for execution, the traders were given direct access to the market through interactive terminals which stop dealers overstepping agreed trading limits and prevent them trading if their cash reserves are too low. Despite the lure of the LIFFE floor only yards away – and the ongoing talk of locals being increasingly unwilling to adapt to electronic trading methods – the 60 positions in Kyte's trading arcade were rented out within days.

The old-style local trader worked on a floor and traded a lot of contracts for a small turn in every trade, often just one tick.[3] The locals were favored in the floor-dealing environment as they could buy and sell without there being a priority on when an order entered a pit. In other words, if the market was 25 bid and 26 offered, the locals, sensing a "paper" (i.e. client/end user) buyer, could quickly jump in and "lift the offer" to get in ahead of the end users. With electronic trading, the methodology of "first in first out" (FIFO) can be employed with ease, thanks to the in-built computer technology. This can be both good and bad. In many open outcry markets the concept of proportional allocations meant that clients often got parts of their orders filled even if they had only recently joined the bid or the offer. Equally, with the new FIFO agenda, much of the advantage previously accorded to locals is eliminated. Their old style of "jobbing" is effectively stunted, if not eliminated entirely. For those locals who are skilled only in the art of jobbing (buying and selling frequently for a very small turn), then oblivion looms in the New Reality.

Dissent in the ranks

However, some floor traders are still doing their utmost to resist the march of progress. In Pakistan, demonstrating floor traders caused a cessation of trading on the floor of the Karachi Stock Exchange during May 1998, in protest at the introduction of screen dealing. It was a reaction not unlike the worst of unionized labor practices – and this was rearing its ugly head at institutions reputedly in the forefront of capitalism. Of course, in their rather self-interested practices throughout much of the post war era, one can make a very strong argument that stock exchanges are in fact defenders of corporatism rather than actually being proponents of free market capitalism per se.

In France that same month, a group of locals attempted to sue the management of MATIF for loss of their livelihoods, following the exchange's move to electronic trading. Ultimately the French authorities paid off all exchange personnel with handsome payouts in line with French government edict.

It is true, the high-handed nature of some exchanges' board's intro-duction of screen trading itself suggested they had not truly grasped the meaning of the New Reality, but traders ought already to have been fully aware of the many failings of these grinding bureau-cracies. Indeed, many of the exchanges to which locals were so keen to cling were

> **Locals must be able to survive in whatever market environments they can find.**

increasingly looking incapable of running organized markets with any form of sensible approach towards innovation.

Nevertheless, the idea that floor traders should receive any recom-pense from an exchange that chooses to remove their pits is utterly misguided. The whole foundation of the derivatives business is a commitment to competitive markets. The MATIF and the Karachi Stock Exchange – and indeed for that matter IPE, SFE, LIFFE, or whoever – all have every right to offer an exchange via floor- or screen-trading methods according to whichever is more efficient. Locals must be able to survive in whatever market environments they can find. The New Reality may frighten many with its social-

Darwinist overtones. However, at no previous time in history has Napoleon's concept of *"la carrière ouverte aux talents"* been a more realistic proposition.

After all, it was floor brokers who at least partially priced themselves out of the market at the same time as many end users (equally short-sightedly) have sought to have brokerage levels reduced to embarrassingly meager levels. In some cases this is inducing a rush to screen trading – which may actually prove to be ill-thought-out in the wake of the next big shock to the system. There is, as we will examine in Chapter 4, a great deal more to going electronic than just dropping several hundred terminals onto assorted desktops around a CBD, switching them on and hoping for the best.

The new 'faceless' environment

"Customers are losing their old-fashioned loyalty to the exchange and are looking more and more at the bottom line. They don't care where they execute deals, as long as it is quick and easy."

Brian Kaye, MD, Fimat (brokerage arm of Société Générale)

Screen-traded markets can do many things very well. However, the screen revolution – while providing cost advantages – does remove the important element of face-to-face "bravado" that helped to make floor trading so efficient. Online markets run the risk of becoming a pale facsimile of their previous floor-traded incarnations. During the late 1980s and early 1990s the sudden disappearance of firm quotations at the first sign of volatility on the Italian screen-traded MIF was the very reason why the pit-traded LIFFE BTP future held a sizable advantage over its Milanese screen-based rival throughout the period from the late 1980s onwards.

So, while screen trading may be dramatically in the ascendant from now on, many markets will have to pay a great deal more attention to just how successful their exchanges are in actually facilitating the trading process. Cheaper and more certain technology does not necessarily mean a better performance, and given that the major screen-based systems have not been proven "under fire" – i.e. in a serious outbreak of volatility – pit traders may yet demonstrate a second wind in the event of a crisis, such as the Exchange Rate Mechanism (ERM) débâcle of 1992 or the stock market crash of 1987.

Equally, the mutterings amongst some market practitioners of late that they have finally routed their local traders are so foolish as to be positively dangerous. Exchanges need liquidity, and it will be the new breed of independent traders who will facilitate trading, be it individuals in tax havens such as the Caribbean or Monaco, or working from large dealing rooms within financial centers, or on the cusp of large conurba-

Locals need exchanges and exchanges need locals.

tions. New technology can be utilized by "old" locals. Moreover, in the New Reality, the screen-based locals can now pay more attention to trading markets traditionally beyond the horizons of their pits, on futures exchanges, in equity markets, and beyond. Locals need exchanges and exchanges need locals. The sooner both parties recognize the merits of change and the ongoing requirement for each party to be involved in the trading process, the sooner the world will be a happier, more liquid place for traders of all shapes and sizes. For locals, it may not be the same as the golden era of open outcry. Nevertheless it will be a place of great opportunity for the correctly oriented trader.

Parallel lives

Perhaps the most significant technological innovation in recent years to emanate from Chicago was the launch of the E-Mini contract in S&P 500 futures on the CME. The S&P 500 tracks the 500 largest stocks in the US and is seen by professionals as a better bellwether of the equity markets than the more commonly discussed Dow Jones Industrial Average which covers a mere 30 shares. However, the large S&P 500 contract size and the innate volatility associated with this heavily traded index tended to drive many smaller traders away from the market. To encourage these smaller traders, the CME opted for a radical route which will have significant repercussions on global capital markets for years to come. Indeed, it will be a cornerstone of the Capital Market Revolution.

Quite simply, the CME launched a "mini" S&P 500 contract, to trade alongside its larger institutional cousin. The E-Mini had a further twist as it was listed not on the CME floor but placed on the GLOBEX system to be traded electronically. Cynics suggested the result would be a loss of liquidity with both products effectively seeing existing business spread between the two markets. Instead, the result was a revelation. A whole new, largely retail-oriented, client base has begun trading the (mini) S&P 500 futures – often via direct electronic interface, usually through the Internet. Secondly, options market makers have found the mini contracts allow them more precise delta hedging.[4] Thirdly, once both instruments had found a modicum of liquidity, there was suddenly an opening for arbitrageurs to step in and ensure that price disparity between the two instruments was minimized. Such parallel markets will have a large role to play in many aspects of capital markets as the revolution gains power. Ironically, the main beneficiaries of the initial arbitrage were the locals on the CME floor who could use screens around the S&P pit to take advantage of data lags in the electronic system to make windfall gains (usually of only a tick or two but with little risk) by trading the mini contract against the bigger product in the pit. Such small lag times may help the "insiders" on the floor for now but gradually as the networks improve, such flaws, biased against the smaller traders will be dramatically reduced. Ironically, much of the time lag is caused by the exchanges floor trade inputters not being able to enter data as fast as the electronic market can deal.

However, the big issue which the E-Mini contracts demonstrated was that a facsimile contract could exist on two different platforms simultaneously (the CBOT has a small sub-division in a room adjacent to the main floor called the "Mid-America Commodity Exchange" ("MidAm") which trades some mini grain and bond contracts, but all are via open outcry). This has big potential repercussions for exchanges. To date it has always been felt that only one market could sustain considerable liquidity in a product. However, in the E-Mini case, an electronic market operated side-by-side with an open outcry system trading similar but differently sized contracts. Theoretically, the electronic market need not be part of the same exchange, so just about anybody could stake a claim to intermediating their market in place of an exchange.

The fact that anybody can now create a means of intermediation to challenge exchanges is of course pivotal to the entire process of the Capital Market Revolution.

Notes

1 Obviously Internet access is slightly slower than direct access through dedicated lines, although the differences are fairly negligible for smaller traders.

2 Clearing agents organize the paperwork/funds transfer/margin payments, etc. between the clearing house and market counterparties.

3 A tick is the smallest quantity open to dealing on a futures floor, usually 0.01 of a basis point for financial contracts, sometimes less. The fact that locals can manage to keep bid–offer spreads for dealing so narrow is a big boon for derivatives markets compared to the stock market. In equities, corporate capital such as market makers have invariably made spreads much wider compared to the derivatives locals.

4 Delta hedging is the process whereby options can be stripped of their directional impetus leaving traders to trade volatility. It is commonplace amongst options for most professionals to spend much if not all of their time trading volatility rather than outright direction.

CHAPTER 3

Teaching old dogs new tricks

Why exchanges need to rethink their relationship with the outside world

"In the future, the stock market will not revolve around brokers, or dealers, or specialists. It will not be limited to the physical location, to a trading floor, even to a central database. The stock market of the future will take place wherever individuals access each other to trade securities. A seat in the stock exchange of tomorrow will be any chair in front of a computer with a modem."

Andrew Klein, founder, Wit Capital Corporation
(issuer of the Internet's first IPO)

A death in the club

The status quo in stock markets is not dead. There is simply no more status quo.

The world's major stock markets have undergone considerable transformation during the past 20 years. Unless they wish to face oblivion, they have a lot further to go yet. In the 1970s and 1980s the stock market "club" broke down. Fixed commissions and other anti-competitive practices were gradually abolished, although many exchanges are still reluctant to permit new practices. When new technology was first mooted, the innate reactionary forces of stock markets across the world balked at change. Such forces remain strong in markets such as New York, where the NYSE holds a tentative grip on the largest stocks but is under increasing fire from the electronic NASDAQ market which has garnered the cream of new technology stocks. A senior exchange official relates a classic story about an Asian exchange, which amply demonstrates the distaste for modern open practices felt not just in this region but throughout the world during recent decades. When a fledgling electronic stock trading system was being operated, the official noted that "the great thing about electronic trading is that it levels the playing field and permits total transparency for all market participants." "Oh well, we certainly don't want that!" replied the Exchange Chairman, somewhat indignant at such an irksome notion as providing every trader with the same information.

With the breakdown of fixed commissions came the breakdown (to a large extent anyway) in the old cartels or other rather unsavory practices that marred some areas of stock market trading. Nevertheless, for all the mutterings about progress with the likes of the "Big Bang" in London's securities trading during 1986, the fact remained that stock trading for those outside the large institutions was essentially a difficult business to enter on remotely equal terms with the other players.

Ironically, it was in a country somewhat removed from the financial mainstream where the biggest upheaval would take place before the revolution was even directly underway. In Sydney the Australian Stock Exchange was created from the disparate regional markets in the major cities of the antipodean continent during the 1980s and within a short period of time it began a nuts-and-bolts reform of the entire dealing process. This involved making stock trading electronic in the mid-1980s and ultimately led to the exchange dropping its membership status and metamorphosing into a "for-profit" corporation listed on its own marketplace on 4 October 1999. The process of going electronic was a harrowing one. Former Information Services Director Rory Collins describes it as being akin to "changing the engines on a Boeing 747 while climbing to 35 000 feet across the mid-Atlantic!".

Nevertheless, everything looked fairly rosy for the club to continue under slightly more competitive pressures through the mid-1980s and early 1990s. The status quo appeared assured.

The lawyer, the brewer, and the case of the very public offering

> "True originality consists not in a new manner but in a new vision."
>
> **Edith Wharton**

Lawyer Andrew Klein probably never expected to become a capital market revolutionary. However, following his much publicized offering for the Spring Street microbrewery, which was issued directly to the public via the Internet, Klein opted to create the first virtual investment bank in cyberspace. Wit Capital Corporation now issues shares on exchanges direct to the public. Such was its success that by early 1999 Klein had to issue apologies to eager Internet investors, riding the high-tech stock boom:

> Wit Capital was founded to level the playing field for the individual investor – to bring our members opportunities and resources once available only to institutions. Please understand that revolutionizing an industry is never easy, but Wit Capital is making significant progress every day, bringing more shares to the public.

To have to make such an apology after a mere couple of years in business was in no way an admission of the failure of the new Wit model. Rather it was a staggering demonstration of just how fast the market was changing. Individual investors were embracing the online culture faster than many existing stock-exchange members could comprehend. For individual traders, news that Wit was adding consid-

Information and price transparency are at the core of the Capital Market Revolution.

erable free research to its Web site for all clients to read was only a final confirmation that the old system of broker research being withheld only for the wealthiest private clients and the institutions was dead. Information and price transparency are at the core of the Capital Market Revolution. The fact that even such leviathans of the securities market as Merrill Lynch began giving away their research (for a "trial period") in late 1999 only serves to emphasize that the markets are now becoming more accessible to retail investors throughout the world.

However, if an online investment bank can offer to sell equities online and a trader can deal in this stock using the Internet, then this begs once again that hoary question of just how much such investment banks are willing to pay for executing business through a particular exchange. With electronic marketplaces such as Tradepoint in the UK able to offer all the facilities of its older and less flexible rival, the London Stock Exchange, we feel it is only a matter of time before the current large exchanges find themselves taking enormous collateral damage from smaller, cheaper, faster markets boasting new technology with minuscule staffs.

A system such as Optimark, which can provide a process of ongoing matching of securities trades in a series of "fixes" during the course of each session, provides the tantalizing possibility of creating an exchange within an exchange. Optimark boasts various processes which create user-satisfaction profiles to match the levels at which counterparties are willing to execute business. Thanks to processes such as Optimark, the stock market of the future – insofar as such formal structures continue to exist – will be a very different animal. Though essentially an auction system for institutions, the benefits of Optimark can be extended to retail traders using amalgamated order books already popular on exchanges such as the Australian Stock Exchange (ASX). By pouring the retail order book into the Optimark system, both institutional and retail clients can match business at fixes that can be as frequent as every few minutes. Goldman Sachs and Merrill Lynch were just two of the 30 leading financial institutions who paid a total of 150 million US dollars to finance the system's development.

In the nineteenth century more than 200 stock exchanges opened in the USA. The invention of the telegraph permitted liquidity to flow to a few fixed marketplaces. The telegraph killed all but a handful of US stock markets. In the Capital Market Revolution the capacity of digital technology to bring together all fixed points to another fixed (or indeed floating) point means that technology of the Internet generation will decimate the world's existing stock exchanges. Fewer than five major stock markets will remain worldwide by 2010. Perhaps two or three of these will be entirely electronic markets which have not yet even been created.

> "Somewhere out there is a bullet with your company's name on it. Somewhere out there is a competitor, unborn and unknown, that will render your business model obsolete."
>
> **Hamel and Sampler, *Fortune Magazine*, 7 December 1998**

The big impetus to adopt as slick a method of technological usage as possible will come from a brokerage cost war that will make the already frenzied rate cuts of the past decade look like a mere bagatelle by comparison. Indeed, in the stock market, those exchanges that are still muddling through with fixed commissions will find their businesses quickly strangled long before the new millennium gets into its stride. If they survive even until 2005 it will be a remarkable achievement. It is startling to recall that even such supposed bastions of capitalism as the London Stock Exchange operated a fixed commission market until the mid-1980s. Fixed commissions will drive exchanges out of business during the Capital Market Revolution. If governments are unable or unwilling to accelerate the deregulation process of financial markets, then deregulated exchanges will simply steal the business from under the noses of the existing bloated cartels that blight a number of economies, most notably in parts of Asia. If a government tries to keep the exchange competition at bay by banning it from existing onshore, it will simply migrate offshore to cyberspace and house its servers in a suitable tax haven.

Inefficient brokers and exchanges have nowhere to hide in the information age.

Inefficient brokers and exchanges have nowhere to hide in the information age. Just as the French revolutionary courts imposed a "reign of terror" with astoundingly bloody consequences, the Capital Market Revolution will be a bloody, life-endangering affair for every reactionary banker's balance sheet. With profits being driven down by decreased revenues, the brokers will have no choice but to sack staff *en masse* in an effort to re-establish equilibrium in the new screen-traded environment. Those brokers whose short-sightedness suggested that getting rid of expensive floor traders would give them respite from the cutting of brokerage rates will find their prospects stymied by an ongoing round of technologically-inspired income reduction. The Capital Market Revolution will give the victors great spoils, but they will be received only by those who have shown the courage to take risks.

Luddites will be doomed in the new millennium. If they have no redeeming skills to be the dealers of the future, then they have no future in the financial markets. The highways and byways of the county of Essex, northeast of London, seems to be clogged with former dealers driving mini-cabs, following unsuccessful attempts to operate independent of the patronage of large commodity and financial institutions in the first wave of deregulation during the late 1980s. There will be a great many more unemployed, for the New Reality requires a much broader skills set than many financial markets personnel have ever considered.

Already, exchanges are falling by the wayside. Take for instance, a commodity that revolves around liquidity, albeit not in the financial markets sense. The London tea market enjoyed weekly auctions in the City of London from 1679 until 1998. The decision to close the market in August 1998 was the result of all the key issues that will increasingly afflict the world's other commodity debt and equity exchanges. Firstly there is the question of geography. The London tea market was a perfectly sensible venture in the late seventeenth century when London was the center of tea drinking, the epicenter of a large empire, and one of very few economically advanced nations on Earth. However, with the product grown overseas in major plantations a considerable distance from London, there was no good reason for the

London tea market to continue to exist. In 1998 the growers in Africa, India, China, and other parts of the world all had access to the Internet. They could create their own deals away from the exchange, over the counter. In the end, the market moved electronic. Dealers are no longer obliged to send their representatives to London for the auctions, and can transact their tea business from their offices on plantations or at importers and exporters throughout the world. The London tea auction was not a major force in world capital markets. However, the ramifications of the move away from a formal face-to-face structure in a fixed location to a decentralized electronic marketplace will ultimately be felt by every exchange, banker, institution, and private individual throughout the world.

At the 1998 London Derivatives Conference, Christopher Sharples concluded the annual debate (where the motion whether exchanges were "enjoying their last few years" had just been narrowly defeated), with the ominous words: *"It is not all over bar the shouting; it is all over, especially the shouting."*

The new borderless perspective

"The stock exchanges of the future will migrate away from the geographical bounds that the interest groups behind any potential European Stock Exchange seek to retain. Instead of a national view, a sector approach is emerging: for example, investors will not view the market in terms of, say, Germany, Sweden or the UK. Instead, their view will be in terms of pharmaceuticals, IT or forest products."

Per E. Larrsson, CEO, OM Group

Sector stock exchanges are a distinct possibility. We can foresee the possibility that the likes of the ASX in Sydney will create a global market for

Sector stock exchanges are a distinct possibility.

resource stocks based around the considerable core competencies of the exchange, which has many domestic resources stocks listed.

Similarly, the high-technology stock market for the world essentially already exists. NASDAQ has garnered so much of the stock traded on the Internet boom as to make it *the* global source of capital for new technology.

With an office overlooking the beautiful opera house created by Charles Garnier in the nineteenth century, Olivier de Montety works in the heart of Paris's centre. Yet for all the classic trappings of the wide boulevards surrounding his office, de Montety is fundamentally a capital market revolutionary. In the city that stormed the Bastille and created the prototype for modern public rebellion, de Montety was one of the core proponents of a very early electronic dealing system. Fimatex was debuted in the late 1980s and had the capacity to provide a small brokerage dealing from anywhere in the world with all the apparatus to become a fully fledged derivatives broker on all the world's exchanges. The system made such a profound impact upon Patrick Young that it helped him decide to leave the brokerage arena for trading. Alas, however, the project was an idea somewhat ahead of its time and despite the backing of the parent FIMAT group (a part of the massive Société Générale banking group), the system never sold a single unit. "The system was simply too early for institutions and too complex for private clients" muses de Montety. Nowadays, however, Fimatex has become a veritable powerhouse in the Capital Market Revolution. De Montety oversees the French arm of its enormous online brokerage operations, increasingly utilizing the Internet but also with order flow from the existing French Minitel network.

Indeed, the French Minitel service is an interesting example of the closed process that is doomed in the information age. The French video text service blossomed during the 1980s as a means of gaining information, booking tickets for all forms of leisure pursuit, and generally providing an excellent tool in the form of a shrunken, less technological version of the Internet. However, once the World Wide Web was born, regardless of the French government's natural interventionist inclination to protect the system, Minitel was already in its death throes, even by the time it had finally opened to the rapidly growing Internet technology. With financial exchanges, it is precisely the same issue. They simply must obey the law of management guru, Peter Drucker: "Sooner or later closed systems have to open up or die."

In the late 1990s open architecture protocol (API) mania swept many exchanges worldwide. However, merely allowing anybody to tack a front-end screen to trade your market will be insufficient. In the New Reality customers are essentially unconcerned with where they transact their business; rather it will be the marketplace that can marry strong liquidity with good, cheap execution and with cheap, secure clearing that will be of greatest importance.

The new merchant princes of capitalism

"Clearing members are asking more and more if we need exchanges. Exchanges have every reason to be worried."

John Damgard, President, FIA

For many years clearing houses had little more than bridal status. Even then, they often expected to go to the altar but were jilted before they got there. Suddenly in the Capital Market Revolution clearing houses are the smartest businesses in town. Interestingly, most clearing houses are already inextricably linked to an existing futures exchange. The only major independent entity at the time of writing (for LIFFE was pursuing it with gusto when this book was being written) was the London Clearing House.

In olden times clearing houses merely operated what traders regarded as a dull but necessary evil. Clearing houses matched every buyer to every seller and guaranteed that, whatever calamities might befall any trader, the counterparty's positions would be safely upheld. Clearing houses guaranteed the standing of locals against the big institutions (and in the case of the collapse of large organizations such as Drexel Burnham Lambert, vice versa). Clearing houses earned a handy stipend for their shareholders but overall their business looked largely unexciting.

However, as the effects of the Capital Market Revolution gather pace, it can be seen that in fact clearing houses are about to enter their golden age. In the New Reality, the clearing house can act as a kingmaker in the financial product food chain, adding much needed credibility in the information age when brands can be created overnight. With the backing of a clearing house, any market mechanism can gain credibility. Moreover, it can be plumbed into the global clearing system without much further ado.

Clearing houses are themselves undergoing something of a radical upheaval. However, uniquely amongst existing institutions facing the Capital Market Revolution, theirs is a situation where the market for their services is primed to explode. At the very core of the futures and options business are the 20 leading exchanges in the world. We

With the backing of a clearing house, any market mechanism can gain credibility.

believe at most six or seven will still be independent in 2010.[1] The bulk of this rationalization will have taken place by 2005. Even as this book is being written, a number of merger talks are in process and several more are rumored. We are not in a position to state which equity or derivatives exchanges will still be in existence by 2010. However, we expect the landscape will be radically changed. For one thing, if the CBOT continues on its current path of self-destruction, then we expect the exchange to be at best a junior partner in a global coalition by the end of the first decade of the new millennium. Certainly, if Chicago loses its dominance as the center of the futures business, the short-sightedness of eschewing common clearing in the late summer of 1998 will likely be seen in the history books as the point where that dominance truly began to unravel.

Similarly, the NYSE has already essentially been bypassed as the key stock market in capitalism's powerhouse, North America. The NYSE will probably survive with its primacy intact for some time yet, as the froth in multimedia stocks meets some resistance. However, the future of the world and therefore the future of world stock markets rests with Microsoft and the other digital media companies. The Dow Jones Industrial Averages served the industrial age, but the likes of Bethlehem Steel or Boeing are not stocks that can be viewed as the future dynamic equities of the world. They have sectoral significance but their glamor days are long over. The future of American equity dealing lies with the likes of NASDAQ, although the NASD needs to keep its act tightly together if it is to avoid being overwhelmed by the new technology and increased promiscuity of exchanges.

In the New Reality a complete minnow of a stock exchange will grow to be a world player. It will be an offshore market and it may be in Bermuda, Jersey, or Singapore, or even a yet-to-be-established cyberspace market with nominal geographical presence in Andorra or Monaco, or perhaps a financial centre within a high tax jurisdiction, such as the Irish Republic; or perhaps a state yet to achieve independence. Remember, in the Capital Market Revolution the status quo no longer exists. To paraphrase the economist Milton Friedman, "any market, anywhere can become a world leader at any time".

> **With virtual dealing in a virtual world, virtual stock trading (using futures) may be the future for many stock traders.**

Meanwhile, in a virtual world, the whole concept of virtual securities dealing may yet take precedence. After all, when stocks are being transferred, the priciest aspect to the whole transaction is the clearing and settlement procedure involving transferring title and storing it in an appropriate depository. Perhaps the solution may be to avoid trading stocks altogether. To date, individual stock futures have yet to make their mark on the capital markets remotely in the size that they should. With virtual dealing in a virtual world, virtual stock trading (using futures) may be the future for many stock traders. After all, the widespread introduction of liquid individual stock futures would create a further form of asset to trade against the option and warrant products, enhancing liquidity in both through greater short selling and spreading opportunity. With dividends increasingly attracting withholding tax at source, investors may become more keen on capital gains in the offshore dealing age emerging from the Capital Market Revolution and ignore dividends entirely, preferring to seek solely capital appreciation through stock futures.

The large equity broking institutions have tended to be trenchantly against individual stock futures (largely out of fear that they could cut their margins on cash stock brokerage). However, the margin on broking equities has already largely disappeared. We believe it will not be long before a major derivatives exchange launches a concerted initiative to trade individual stock futures. Once such an initiative is successfully established, it will cause several large stock markets to wither and die as they will not be able to cope with the dynamic competition to be found in the derivatives business. Moreover, we expect the biggest link-ups in the future will come from futures exchange – stock-market tie-ups. By mid 1999 a series of such mergers, in the wake of the DTB-Deutsche Börse initiative some time earlier, were under way. The linkage of the likes of the Hong Kong Futures Exchange with its corporatist local stock market equivalent showed little sign of understanding the New Reality. The proposed merger of SIMEX and the Singapore Stock Exchange looked more interesting with the potential for the SSE's vast private client business to get better access to derivatives markets being a largely unmentioned but potentially very attractive element of the deal – providing existing constraints within the GLOBEX alliance did not hamper technology platform saving the other structural cost reductions. Perhaps most interesting of all, the Sydney Futures Exchange, having initially agreed a deal with the Australian Stock Exchange, found itself being bid for by the share registry software company Computershare. In the first public battle between quoted companies for a futures exchange, it was clear that Computershare recognized the benefits of creating its own exchange not just for derivatives, but also for equities, out of the SFE's existing infrastructure. Meanwhile the prospects for a market such as NASDAQ to be linked with a major derivatives market outside the USA for instance would create a powerhouse exchange that would have clear global potential, a broad product range, and huge potential to dominate large chunks of the securities markets.

While many leviathans will go out of business, there will in fact be vastly more derivatives exchanges in the world than at present. For in the future, using electronic trading mechanisms, there will be much more opportunity to create exchanges to deal in small global or even regional niches. For example, environmental trading will grow steadily in the next millennium – already in 1998 there were several exchanges staking a claim to this business, including the OM venture based in Edinburgh and the IPE in London – as well as New York, Chicago, and Sydney. Equally, weather derivatives are set to be an enormous growth area for the next decade. We also believe the increasing globalized commoditization of insurance will result in considerable growth in insurance contracts by 2005. We cover new and expanding markets in greater depth in Chapter 9.

Every new exchange will need a clearing house. Since costs of establishing new ones are a major burden to new market structures (which are otherwise remarkably low in capital requirements compared to the old people-dominated structures) the use of an existing clearing house will be a much simpler solution. Increasingly, clearing houses will also be expanding their remit beyond the futures and options exchanges. New model stock markets will more frequently utilize a clearing house to facilitate settlement. The London Tradepoint Stock Exchange, established in 1995, already employs the London Clearing House in precisely this role. With the power to bestow financial credibility on markets at their whim, clearing houses will increasingly have the capacity to bless financial markets or blight them in a manner akin to the medieval *droit de seigneur*.

Meanwhile, there is also the possibility that clearing houses can actually even threaten the very existence of the exchanges they have been serving for hundreds of years. As credit concerns mount across the world, the clearing of OTC-traded instruments will undoubtedly gather pace (it was first undertaken by OM in Sweden in the 1980s but has made relatively little progress since). However, if OTC clearing takes off, the situation is likely to arise where the clearing house will find itself selling its services to end users in competition (at least in some ways) to the exchanges who wish to get more business on their markets. Frankly, the prognosis in such encounters for exchanges looks bleak. Increasing simplicity of access and more onerous regulation of exchanges has continued to push business on to OTC markets in many financial centers for a decade or more. Settling such transactions through clearing houses will gather momentum as more and more microbanks and other Internet-based virtual financial counterparties begin trading with greater gusto.

Regulators in revolt and at war

"Now our basic philosophy is to get out of the way while still providing investor protection."

Arthur Levitt Jr., Chairman, Securities and Exchange Commission

For the past few decades, financial markets have been a wonderful plaything for governments. Managing economies has become altogether more dangerous and difficult because of globalization and the increasing power of the market to recognize politicians' economic follies. However, in financial markets, governments have been able to do their utmost to provide a structure that makes them feel as if they are doing something of benefit. Whilst occasionally there have been benefits, in most cases the result has been little more than a strangulation of natural capitalist processes. In London the salaries for compliance officers have soared, as companies have had to comply with a never-ending stream of regulatory edicts, many of which demonstrate a palpable lack of understanding of financial markets by the professionals allegedly employed to facilitate a safe and sensible organization. Compliance chiefs in London are not known as "business prevention officers" without reason. The end result has been a sprawling bureaucracy that still does not protect investors from determined fraudsters and leaves the innocent majority largely hamstrung in their attempts to deal effectively. Brokers have been hit hard. With income squeezed through continuing discounting, increased regulatory costs have been an unwelcome burden.

> **With income squeezed through continuing discounting, increased regulatory costs have been an unwelcome burden.**

Almost all practitioners would agree that some form of regulation is a necessary evil for financial markets. However, in recent years that regulation appears to have gone too far. Now it is likely to snap in precisely the opposite direction. For, while regulators may claim that they understand the dynamics of the Internet (they don't), that they can operate their regulatory regimes within their geographical boundaries with regard to the Internet (they can't), and that their remit will go unchallenged (it won't), the truth is that their very existence is under threat.

The behavior of some regulators towards the virtual world of finance almost defies belief. In the UK the Financial Services Act of 1985 has been used as a rather crude cudgel against any form of Internet-based financing that does not appeal to the UK regulators. One of their more frightening proclamations has been to claim that any investment scheme offered by a corporation beyond a current major regulatory regime is being offered to British investors simply by dint of being reported in English. While English may be the global language of financial markets, apparently this nonetheless makes it a threat to the UK investors. When a senior UK regulator was asked why he would not amend this ridiculous claim, the tart reply was that it was up to a trading organization to get their counsel to reinterpret the Act and that at this stage the UK regulator would look benignly on such an interpretation. Quite why brokers and end-users are supposed to spend their money to dig the UK regulators out of a hole of their own making was not explained.

The simple fact is that single-nation regulators are largely dead in the water. There will be increasing levels of globalized regulatorial co-operation but the scope and size of domestic regulatory regimes is likely to shrink vastly in the next decade. Frankly, this will be no bad thing. Regulators need to understand the changing nature of the trading business. Alas, their lack of grasp of dynamics thus far suggests there is relatively little hope for most of their bureaucrats. Any heavy-handedness at this stage of the Capital Market Revolution by bureaucrats will merely have massive repercussions. The American government's increasingly swingeing regulations during the 1960s resulted in a massive offshore shift of expatriate US dollars to create the London-based Eurodollar market. Similar pig headedness by regulators in the modern age will result in a migration to another jurisdiction at the speed of light.

Interestingly, in the USA, there have been increasing signs of regulators at the SEC and the CFTC taking a greater interest in softly-softly tactics, which seems to suggest that they may have an eye on becoming regulators for the entire online world. Certainly a very light degree of regulation would be a boon for many firms. However, even with America's status as sole superpower, it will find gunboat diplomacy difficult to enforce in the online world.

> In the New Reality, governments cannot expect to dominate markets as they did with their domestic exchanges.

Certainly, regulators' biggest problem in years to come will be regulatory arbitrage – the process whereby markets move offshore to create a parallel market to the onshore variant. The Swedish OM market did precisely this with the opening of OMLX in the 1980s when the Swedish government played with withholding tax introduction. The OMLX market traded without the tax constraints and the Swedish government had to back down. In the New Reality, governments cannot expect to dominate markets as they did with their domestic exchanges.

Trying the new model on the old

London's Stock Exchange appears largely bewildered by the dynamics of the Capital Market Revolution, stumbling into an alliance with the Deutsche Börse in mid-1998. On Wall Street, even when the AMEX was subsumed into the electronic NASDAQ, the NYSE appeared in denial at the prospects for electronic trading. In Tokyo, the giddying collapse in stock prices was still uppermost in the minds of the stockmarket authorities there. In some ways we suspect the Deutsche Börse may have been sold a bad deal, as the promiscuity of London's dealers may yet result in them moving *en masse* to a rival market. Certainly, it would be difficult to have much faith in the London Stock Exchange's policy, as it is largely impossible to see what their policy has been for the past 20 years or so. Indeed, the London Stock Exchange cannot be accused of having lost the plot, since it is difficult to see when they actually had a firm grasp of the plot in the first place.

Somewhat ironically, therefore, the first stock exchange to attempt to remodel its processes has not been a major market but rather the ASX. Headquartered in Sydney, the ASX was entirely remodeled in the late 1990s. Options were the final open-outcry market to move to screens in 1997, 12 years after stocks had migrated from the trading floor. An Internet-based venture capital scheme was attempted, although it was at best sluggish in its initial year – most probably as a result of the bureaucracy that onshore regulation appears to attract. Having taken up a profit-seeking status, CEO Richard Humphreys persuaded the Australian government to pass through enabling legislation to permit the exchange to list its shares on its own market. Brokers were instantly rewarded overnight with huge gains in their shares which replaced their previous membership holdings. In the short term the stock market gained ground; in the longer term it may have difficulty holding its share.

The ASX's move was a very interesting one, particularly as the ASX was probably one market which could at least survive a few years longer than its mainstream opposition before being dented by the New Reality. Nevertheless, as a for-profit entity, the ASX is an interesting example in the remodeling of an exchange. ASX is essentially set with its core stock-dealing operations and an options offshoot, ready to do business in the global frontier. Its long history of dealing in resources stock and its strong record of avoiding many scandals and shady operators (unlike the other big gold/resources stock market in Vancouver, for instance whose reputation is less strong) could give ASX the pole position if it mounted a bid to become the world's leading exploration and mining exchange (in the same way that technology stocks seem almost naturally to migrate to America's electronic NASDAQ these days). The only market from which the ASX had yet to release value at the time of writing was its clearing house. However, this could come in handy for leverage during the negotiations with the SFE.

Vertical or horizontal integration?

While many exchanges are rightly concerned about the possible impact of a single European currency, it is foolish not to prioritize the need for common clearing. While OTC players will talk about side-stepping clearing houses, a clearing house process is still better from a risk-management standpoint than an endless morass of counterparty agreements and offsets. Clearing houses may look to differentiate credit standing in the future, and provided this does not make entry level requirements prohibitive – so pushing smaller traders out of the business entirely – we do not believe this is a bad way to go.

Suddenly the whole focus of exchanges looks dangerously out of kilter with the *realpolitik* of the capital markets business. The increasing disintermediation will make the exchanges increasingly liable to outright redundancy, while the clearing houses have the capacity to take on a new role that could make them the masters of much of the trading universe.

The Capital Market Revolution may not take any prisoners, but it will see the sort of slashing and burning that has been unknown in financial markets throughout the past three hundred years.

Notes

1 The GLOBEX alliance based around the GLOBEX 2 system, launched in early 1999 already sees three leading exchanges, CME in Chicago, MATIF in Paris and Singapore's SIMEX, co-operating widely and perhaps providing a prelude to a merger.

CHAPTER 4

The perils of transition

How the revolution can kill you

> "Whosoever desires constant success must change with the times."
> **Niccolo Machiavelli**

Plus ça change

MATIF had been born in Paris, France, in 1986 at the height of François Mitterrand's socialist presidency – with his blessing. In many countries it would seem ironic to have such a bastion of capitalism created under such a left-wing regime (which had prided itself on widespread nationalization only a few years earlier). In any case, Mitterrand cannily went on to privatize in his second term much of what he had nationalized in his first.

MATIF quickly established itself trading French government bonds, interest rates, and stock futures. There were forays into commodity products and a very successful niche in options. Exchange options volumes have always been much higher pro rata to futures in Paris than on much larger exchanges such as LIFFE in London. Indeed, during the late 1980s MATIF even edged ahead of LIFFE in overall volumes. However, LIFFE successfully diversified beyond the UK market place while MATIF remained a healthy but domestic exchange (although with the globalization of trading, naturally it had end users throughout the world).

MATIF was the first European exchange to launch a big push towards being a core player in the EMU derivatives, born after 1 January 1999. Sensing the move to cost-effective screen-trading measures, and keenly aware that the Globex system would have been an unmitigated disaster without MATIF's participation in the after-hours market mechanism developed by Reuters, Globex 2 was to be housed on a platform developed by the Société de Bourse Française (SPF – the Paris Stock Exchange and MATIF's parent). Sensing an opportunity to carve itself a reputation in history as the first market to switch from open outcry to electronic trading as its primary means of dealing, MATIF lunged headlong into a whirlwind period of six months which almost spelt disaster for the Paris market.

We are the "big swinging elbows"

On 23 July 1998 a frenzy of selling rocked MATIF. After a relatively quiet session, suddenly orders flooded into the French Government Bond futures contract (known as the "Notionnel"). Official MATIF correspondence outlined the incident as follows:

> At 4.12 p.m. on Thursday, July 23, the NSC trading system received over 100 fill-or-kill sell orders at market price for the September 1998 delivery month of the Notional contract from the order-management server (SLE) of a member based in London. On this occasion, over 230 transactions representing a total of some 12 500 contracts were executed in the space of two minutes. As a result, the price fell by some 150 basis points to 103.61 before the market recovered to set the price back at 105.10, the level prevailing prior to the incident.
>
> In the following minutes, 13 members contacted CESAME (center for supervision and assistance on the electronic market) to request the cancellation of 114 trades representing a total of 4 462 contracts in accordance with the provisions of article 2.3.4 and following of the Official Instruction, Market Organization – Trading Procedures.

When the selling abated, the market bounced back rapidly to the earlier levels.

Rumors of hacking abounded. One trader remarked that "the whole Paris futures community is shocked by what happened." A letter to MATIF members from the exchange CEO Pascal Samaran began:

The incident which occurred on July 23 has caused considerable concern among market participants who understandably want to know the reasons for the abrupt fall in the Notional future that day and how it could have happened. This has given rise to much comment, not all of it well-informed.

Confidence in MATIF and its management slumped. The counter-party who had initiated the trades attempted to deny all knowledge of the orders being anything to do with them. An enquiry was immediately instituted, with Cap Gemini and Kroll O'Gara jointly placed in charge of making a report to the market on behalf of both the counterparty and the exchange. The results were little short of astounding. Or rather, terrifying.

What about hacking?

Sooner or later the law of averages dictates hacking is bound to happen. However, fortunately, the relatively lax security evidenced by computer networks and Web sites belonging to certain military and governmental organizations the world over has kept the world's hacking fraternity happy. Nevertheless, the whole issue of somebody hacking on to an exchange is perfectly plausible.

Thankfully, the world's leading exchanges take the threat posed by hackers seriously. After all, the possibility of fiscal losses would be huge. However, arguably more important would be the threat of loss of business from dwindling confidence in that particular market. In the increasingly competitive era of the Capital Market Revolution, the prospect of the first exchange to be successfully hacked and going out of business as a result, is highly probable.

A potential hacker is likely to be either:

- a disgruntled employee of the exchange, or a counterparty – most likely one skilled in technology, or having recently worked in the technology department;
- an outside hacker trying to make a large media splash (as mentioned above, until various arms of government and the military industrial complex raise their security significantly, it is unlikely that the world of mammon will find itself a major target for most hackers – but it will only take one such person to get under the wire).

The prospect of a hacker entering a screen-trading system is one too truly terrifying in its ramifications for financial markets to contemplate. If, for instance, a counter-party claims a hacker is at play and unilaterally chooses not to own up to trades

▶

taken in its name, what should be the appropriate response from an exchange, or indeed a clearing house?

There is also the equally valid question of where an exchange's liability begins and ends with regard to an order in its system. For instance, when an order is entered into a remote broker's terminal at a third party's office, can it be the exchange's liability? If an order is still on the broker's LAN when it gets somehow speared, amended, or added to, who precisely is liable? True, logic dictates that the answer here is not the exchange's problem. However, if a counterparty screams "hacker" loud enough, will the media and other market counterparties be able to discern that the problem was not the responsibility of the exchange? With financial markets remaining susceptible to rumors, the prospect of hacker claims doing immeasurable damage not merely to one exchange but indeed the whole financial system is considerable. Even the merest claim of a hacker was enough to dent confidence at least temporarily in exchanges in Frankfurt and Paris during the second half of 1998.

Even if an order is the responsibility of an exchange only when it reaches that market's system, there are still points to ponder. Is that linkage at the point the order enters an ISDN line from the counterparty/broker direct to the market? Or is it when it enters the brokers' own physical building? Must an order be in the exchange server before it can be said to have been hacked at the exchange's risk? Nobody seems too clear on this topic at present. And it is surely worrying that lawyers and assorted bloodsuckers will sooner or later reap their own little monopoly profit from the financial markets.

With a system such as PATS one can largely delineate responsibility and where it lies – i.e. with the trader, the clearer, or the exchange, through an embedded audit trail. However, some brokers are so concerned about this potential problem and the sanctity of their database that they believe only proprietary technology is the way to go. One such person is Australian Joe Cross, whose United Capital Securities benefits not merely from the patronage of some of Rupert Murdoch's interests but has also developed its own product for trading derivatives both on dedicated screens with direct telephone lines and through the Internet. As Cross describes his operation: "We are a technology company which provides brokerage services." That in essence is the new model broker.

For exchanges, the situation is a dreadful dilemma. Once one party is seen to get away with a trade that is reputedly due to hacking, then other participants are – in effect – going to be encouraged to put forward such excuses for (what is most likely going to be) a simple order-inputter's error. The prospect of an entire breakdown in electronic financial markets follows logically from the domino effect of participants claiming (whether legitimately or not) that their trade entry has been affected by hacking.

The mystery of workstation 201

The smart money was on "human error" being to blame. Nevertheless, with the counterparty denying any error on their part, MATIF went through several months of severe media scrutiny. This error had been the latest (and largest) of several that had severely dented market confidence. In the end the affair created a series of simple blueprints that management ought to consider as being a good way to avoid such foibles in future.

Ultimately, when the report was issued, the egg ended up on the counterparty's face. It transpired that Salomon Smith Barney, one of the biggest and supposedly most brilliant of American investment banks, had in fact sold over 10 000 Notionnel Bond futures, thanks to the sort of elementary error which if it were the centerpiece of a plot in a thriller everybody would discard as being too ridiculous to be true. In the 1980s Salomons had been portrayed by former employee Michael Lewis in a rather unflattering light. Lewis' book *Liar's Poker* was famous for bringing the Salomon Brothers' mantra "we are the big swinging dicks" to public prominence. Remarkably, this time around it was "the big swinging elbow" that brought Salomon Brothers back into the limelight.

Substantial forensic examination of Workstation 201 showed there had been nothing wrong with the terminal except an inadvertent human input that had begun the wild trading swing. The culpable factor on the MATIF NSC-VF terminal was the F12 key, which permitted a 'lean' to become somewhat of a new-fangled 'lien' in financial markets. If double clicked, this key would instantly enter an order, regardless of magnitude. Admittedly, Salomons could clutch at one straw which was that an upgrade to the NSC software had not been implemented on their system (which was at the Salomon Brothers International Limited offices in London). This upgrade from version 4.10 to 4.10a would have eliminated the dangers of the "double F12" functionality and had been available since 1 July 1998.

The independent report included a gem of an excuse from the hapless "trader" who had sold the 10 000 lots:

> "We've done all these because we were on another screen and leaning against the keyboard and I guess we were trading."
> **The voice of the SBIL trader on the Salomon Brothers' tapes**

Meanwhile, as the investigators were gathering their information regarding that fateful Notionnel trading session in late July, that most famous of ex-Salomon Brothers trading supremos, John Merriwether, was occupying the limelight with news that his Long-Term Capital Management Hedge Fund had essentially achieved the fiscal equivalent of biodegrading. It was not a classic month for a bank widely regarded as being a generally crack outfit amongst the world's derivatives élite. Even with the benefit of hindsight, it remains difficult to say anything without adding to Salomon Brothers' already considerable embarrassment.

In open outcry markets errors are essentially always transparent. The fact that one commits an error in front of several dozen (or possibly hundred) counterparties, means that frequently it is easy to see the follies of traders in the pits. This has also meant that in many instances traders would be forgiven certain errors and the trades canceled. However, with screen trading, the conspiracy theorists can have a field day as on most occasions there is little transparency as to what has happened. If the bank claims not to have inputed the trades, as was the case with Salomons Brothers, then it is difficult to do anything other than undergo a lengthy and detailed forensic inquiry. However, the resulting weeks of wait only serves to harm confidence in the market in the first place.

The fact is that in transparent markets, wrongdoers need to be transparent in their actions and named where they have endeavored to evade any possible degree of responsibility, no matter how unjust this charge may be. Without such market transparency, exchange derivatives trading disclosures could become as murky as those on many stock exchanges (which are notoriously lacking in transparency and liquidity compared to their derivatives cousins). While there are many stock markets where it is seen as a good thing that transparency is kept to a minimum to permit "block trades", we really find this very difficult to stomach. The more information is withheld from a trader, the more an information élite is created. The purpose of information-dense resources such as computers is to permit all parties to trade with equal access to price. To restrict access to information and trading is to miss the very crux of the information change driving the Capital Market Revolution.

> The more information is withheld from a trader, the more an information élite is created.

Interestingly, the MATIF allowed (in compliance with the existing exchange rules), the opportunity for trades in this error to be canceled if both counterparties agreed. Rumors abounded of rather panicked calls from Salomons staff seeking to cancel as many orders as possible. However, from an executed error total of some 10 607 contracts Sallies ended up having to "wear" (i.e. keep) some 10 488. Presumably, the rumors were as erroneous as the claim that a hacker did the trades in the first place.

The new frontiers of risk[1]

Way back when, life really was an awful lot simpler. You see in those days we all stood in big pits in the middle of a floor and shouted ourselves silly. When things went wrong, there was always a tangible way to see what was happening.

There were of course errors and some went into the annals of floor-trading history as epics of incompetence. There was the floor trader who on his way out for a tea break called over a junior trader (in a pit where business was fairly moribund that day) and whispered "sell 500 at market." By the time the senior trader had returned from his coffee, the hapless junior dealer had sold something like 275 lots (against all odds). The loss wasn't remotely as painful as it might have been, although it was enough to earn a rebuke from the company's Managing Director which, so far as we are aware, was anatomically invalid, but let's not digress…

Then of course there was the trader who was asked to do a purchase and sale of

▶

one lots in the foreign currency futures which were a rather unsuccessful feature of LIFFE's early years. The trader promptly walked into the pit and bought one lot from the offer and sold one lot to the bid several ticks away. Had he of course used the (permissible on LIFFE) "crossing" procedure, he could have done both lots at the same price in the middle of the bid/offer spread. To this day, the trader concerned is affectionately known as "Deutschmark" by all and sundry who ever graced the floor, even if only for a few months.

When LIFFE was in the Royal Exchange Building there was a pressing need for space in the latter months of the exchange's tenure in this historic building. This meant that often the smaller pits at the end of the floor nearest the viewing gallery would from time to time be shuffled around. In one memorable instance during the late 1980s the Bund pit (then a rising star of the futures contract firmament) was moved and enlarged, swapping places with the FTSE 100 stock index futures pit.

One poor soul of a pit broker returned from a three-week holiday and was handed an order selling a considerable quantity of Bunds. Meanwhile, the pits had been juggled in the midst of his holiday and his colleagues had forgotten to tell him of the pit swap. Anyway, not having a regular trader in the Bunds at this stage, the broker in question wandered into the FTSE pit and merrily sold a hundred or more Bunds. Then, as he was looking at the folk around him (the FTSE pit was generally slightly older on average than the financial pits, largely because many redundant or otherwise "ex-dividend" stockbrokers had turned to being futures locals to earn a crust), he made the fateful second error of his morning's work.

"Er, this is the Bund pit?" he asked while busily writing counterparty details on his trading card. Merciless to a fault, the locals promptly ramped the market up about 30 ticks on the back of this poor broker's return from what turned out to be perhaps the most expensive holiday of his life.

So, floor trading had its errors, but now those ways are being stamped out by the all-pervasive methods of screen dealing. As we know, screens have lovely audit trails. Or at least they do once anybody actually enters trades into a system. The risks remain that there could be extensive manipulation planned before orders are entered. Anyway, the fundamental wisdom suggests screen dealing is vastly safer than open outcry.

In this case, as in so many others, the fundamental wisdom sucks. True, screen trading cuts out a great many foibles, but the idea that screen dealing removes all risks is utterly wrong. Thanks to human ingenuity, there are literally endless possibilities for traders to create new error types thanks to the wonderful innovations of new technology.

The classic Salomons Notionnel Bond error of 23 July 1998 (the day of "the big swinging elbow") ushered in a whole new arena for trading errors which over the next few years will cause many an established firm to blush, and may even result in some being unable to play the game any more. Controversial? Yes. Unreasonable? No. Possible? Well … it never ceases to amaze us the ingenious ways traders can lose money utilizing new technology. Even in the short duration of the Capital Market Revolution to date we have already seen lots of them.

Take Juan Pablo Davilla, Chief Futures Trader at Codelco, the Chilean state-owned copper company, who entered a few trades incorrectly on his computer in early 1994 and discovered he had all of a sudden lost some 30 to 40 million US dollars. With some judicious escalation he managed to rack the loss up to 200 million dollars (or about 0.5 percent of Chile's then GDP) before he got caught.

Many brokers will recall how the fax was hailed as a great invention as it facilitated sending confirmations from Chicago T Bonds night session to London overnight without the need for a cumbersome telex machine. Of course, like all electronic gismos, fax is only as good as its operator. When the pertinent broker forgot to look at the fills sheet one day, he promptly missed a hundred-lot stop-order fill on a late session price spike, which subsequently cost the company 63 000 US dollars when the mess was sorted out nearly two weeks later. Pretty stupid? Yes. Impossible that such stupidity could happen in today's market? Well, we don't share your optimism.

You see, the new frontiers of risk are in fact much less tricky than all those VaR sums that so transfix many aspects of the risk community. Indeed, a little judicious good management in the next few years will go a long way to saving many institutions from some very embarrassing loss situations in the future. Not merely financial losses but also losses of credibility arising from stupidity in the workplace.

The whole risk business is fascinating, fabulous, and also missing out on a heap of big risks to hand at this moment. It's not systemic, it's not volatility, it's the fact that thousands of overcrowded trading positions all over the world are being further filled up with workstations that actually do live trades. They don't commit things to brokers, or send modifiable messages to the back office. These little monsters transmit your orders instantly to the market itself and, before you realize what's what, you've traded. Now, true enough there are those little "version 4.10a" amendments that don't let you trade willy nilly all the time without confirmation. However, all these systems can be overridden or turned off in some way, shape, or form. Ultimately a series of keys can be hit accidentally. Yes, it's less likely than the single keystroke error, but happen it will. On the law of averages alone, given how many keystrokes take place all over the world on financial market computers every day, there will be errors, and many will appear downright hilarious in retrospect.

On the EUREX system, two sessions run simultaneously. A live session is actually trading for real money, while for training traders or demonstration purposes, a simulation session operates adjacent to the real money environment. Now, you can tell what's coming, can't you? Well, actually, it has already happened. Despite the fact that one needs different passwords to access live trading as opposed to the simulated session (and both screens look distinctly different), there has been at least one recorded incident of a trader being aggressive in the real market when he thought he was playing on the "sim." session.

The precise comments of the Managing Director are not known, although one version was somewhat scatological.

There are whole hordes of new risk types out there waiting for an error to discover them. Food wasn't permitted on the LIFFE floor but one can certainly have it close to computer terminals in offices across the globe. Now, with the exception of Britain's first true mass-market PC, the Sinclair ZX80/81 series of the early 1980s, PC keyboards are largely allergic to having consumables applied to their input function-ality. We reckon food and drink errors will begin growing exponentially in the early years of the new millennium. Sooner or later somebody is going to drop coffee on their keyboard. Indeed, Patrick Young used to have a colleague at one London brokerage whose contribution to the dealing room seemed to revolve around little more than frequently emptying a nice sugary cup of scalding hot caffeine over a Reuters Schwarzatron keyboard. Or rather a seemingly never-ending stream of replacement Schwarzatron keyboards.

The keyboard risk arena is so multi-faceted that there is probably a chapter's worth of analysis just looking at all the different potential scenarios. However, the main two are:

- keyboard gets liquid/food inside it and shorts out, sending a "phantom order" signal to the PC itself and on to the market – not a pleasant prospect ...;
- in a frantic effort to clean the keyboard the trader gets the right sequence of key punches into the system and is trading like wildfire – prospect: arguably even worse.

There are also subtle twists, like the trader who empties coffee over their keyboard and then turns it upside down to let the fluid run out, all the time trapping a couple of trading keys in maximum attack mode. Yes, there will be some template add-ons to try and eliminate this but they won't prevent every situation. And we haven't touched leaving things on keyboards such as books, rulers, coats, pens, etc., etc. The biggest dangers are posed by the cheapest pieces of stationers' supplies. Rest assured, before too long an errant paper clip in a suitable jam will ratchet up one of the more significant open positions in a dealing room. True, it may take a few terrorist revolutionary paper clips working in unison to achieve maximum impact, but judging from the clutter that affects many dealers' desks that prospect is not far away.

Cleaner risk will sooner or later claim a few hundred lots of electronic trade as a brisk brush over the keyboard makes a market with gusto. Ironically, the screen display may actually be turned off by the time of cleaning, so the cleaner will go home blissfully unaware of their market prowess. Admittedly traders have to log in electronically to access their trading screens, but not all of them always log off, no matter how often they are reminded. In any case, the cleaning might be during "Chicago hours" in London when the terminals are still on and the trader is off at the coffee machine (see also "caffeine risk" above).

Meanwhile, the risk henceforth referred to as "Bloomberg spread risk" will soon hit a headline somewhere. Hector will be quietly seeking his usual cash-and-carry arbitrage ratios on the computer and will gently punch the appropriate keys on the keyboard, all the while wondering why the mouse isn't on the screen (if he isn't oblivious to the mouse altogether). Soon, Hector will either give up spread searching in frustration or discover that he needed the keyboard to the left of the one that is now happily selling GLOBEX Eurodollars.

Meanwhile, electronic toys such as Furbies have become the bane of dealing rooms, as their electronic communication pulse can in fact harm the workings of certain computer equipment, causing all sorts of nasty skews in the trading and risk management process. "Plus ça change, plus c'est le même risque …"

The whole issue of trading risks has been blessed with an entire paradigm shift that will be unpleasant for many. Nevertheless errors will still occur. Sheathing keyboards in plastic may help, but fluids are stubborn and the human brain has a capacity to get around even the most logically established of risk procedures. A bloodbath of new error types is looming out there.

On the floor everybody could witness your error and a general consensus would frequently save traders from their own foibles. However, in the brave new world of screen trading, where dealers cannot see each other, the fraternity of face-to-face dealing will make such a forgiving attitude more difficult to permit without an aura of suspicion arising, as has already occurred at the MATIF in the early transition stages of their system. When the TIFFE launched its online system over ten years ago, on the first day's trading an operative entered a front month order in a back month and traded immediately at a price in Euroyen that was a good 100 basis points away from the correct price for that month. The hapless trader was made to wear his error. In the rest of the world, pretty much everybody was amazed at this inscrutably Japanese solution to a problem. It seemed at best incredibly harsh, at worst pretty daft.

Today we can actually see how right the TIFFE was. As a leading exchange CEO told Patrick Young a few months ago, the difficulty with screen trading is how to stop a dealer from entering a speculative trade of several hundred lots and then, if the position doesn't work out, calling central market control and asking for the position to be cancelled, as it was an "error." How can we prove it was an error and not just a "punt" that went wrong? How indeed. As Patrick told the CEO in no uncertain terms, there are players in some markets who would try to exploit any flexibility in what is an error and what isn't. Market confidence will be paramount in the electronic age and we suspect a lot of traders will find themselves wearing transparent errors from which they would have escaped in open outcry but to which they will be held accountable in the electronic age. Certainly, exchanges will have to think long and hard about kerb procedures and the like in this new era, as otherwise traders will lose confidence. It looks as if wearing losses in the TIFFE style is more likely to be the norm than the old open outcry system where losses could be forgiven as the whole pit had seen what went wrong.

In the case of many if not most of the errors outlined above, a simple filter on orders would prevent them. In the case of the big swinging elbow, Salomons had apparently not thought through the ramifications of electronic trading activity. This was a failure on the part of both dealing and systems management. Increasingly institutions will favor intelligent front-end systems with in-built risk controls such as PATS or Trading Technologies. Nevertheless, the safety catch on a pistol is only any use if it has been properly configured.

There may be a lot of funny error stories to come but the "new frontiers of risk" are deadly serious.

The new modalities of screen trading open up a whole host of potential pitfalls for the trading of markets. Sooner or later we expect to see a judiciously dropped cup of coffee short-circuiting a keyboard and so leading to another order entry error (although perhaps not of the order of magnitude as that exercised by Salomons' "big swinging elbow").

The exchanges are likely to tighten up on order entry errors, for the problem now overhanging the market is one where big houses could buy/sell large clips and then, if the position doesn't work out, claim an error and have the trades busted. Alternatively, if the trade goes well, then they will be able to profit. Such a trade happened when the screen-based TIFFE was opened in Tokyo in 1989. A trader dealt in the wrong month, placing an order out of line with the market. It was instantly executed and the TIFFE management made the bank wear the instant loss (of 100 000 US dollars) in order to encourage an orderly market. At the time, many brokers thought this sheer madness. Nowadays, with screen-traded markets prone to manipulation by large dealers who can cry "wolf" if their position goes against them, the likelihood is that brokers and dealers will have to be very careful what orders they enter as the market will want to see them making good on all entered orders.

Meanwhile, brokers who have simply looked at the up-front cost savings of the move to screen trading may be terrified to find that suddenly they are wearing a lot more error positions than previously could be easily canceled, or removed on the "kerb" in an open outcry market.[2]

MATIF's brave new world

"Electronic trading is not the end of human intervention in the trading process and I believe some good sense doesn't hurt anybody."

Pascal Samaran, CEO, MATIF

The Salomons affair was the final and largest crisis of a series of problems that had afflicted the MATIF exchange during the previous six months. For MATIF was going through the incredible upheaval of being the first derivatives exchange in the world to go from total open outcry to total screen trading. By comparison, the much vaunted "Big Bang" in London's stock exchange in 1986 had merely seen the floor closed down and the dealers move upstairs to a marketplace where market makers showed quotations on screens but dealing was still carried out by a broker telephoning one of the market makers. This sort of passive system was not a great success, since it largely robbed the market of liquidity and transparency. Hence London's decision to move itself towards a quote-driven computerized system in 1997 was seen by many dealers as a first step towards the possibility of a liquid stock market which would encourage less corporatism and give private capital more chance of playing the game.

At MATIF members were interested in seeing a period of parallel dealing where dealers could use either pits or the NSC electronic system. Although members wanted to see a phased introduction of technology, Jean-François Théodore, the new MATIF Chairman, apparently decided MATIF would go screen-based in a headlong all-encompassing lunge. So parallel trading came in with the market having a full complement of several hundred terminals available immediately, in a number of different locations including London as well as Paris.

> **MATIF officials and members alike were stunned by the migration of business from floor to screen within a staggeringly short period of time.**

MATIF officials and members alike were stunned by the migration of business from floor to screen within a staggeringly short period of time. The first parallel session was in early April. By the end of May, MATIF announced a move to exclusively electronic trading. The cost-pressures to use screens was just too great. Somewhere between 600 and 700 floor staff lost their jobs to the new technology.

Market practitioners in Paris universally liked the new NSC system with VF for futures and VO for options. The whole transition looked like a stunning success. The NSC hardware is tough, reliable and user friendly. It also doesn't tend to hold on to orders or go slow. But, as ever, there were some hiccoughs to be sorted out.

Difficult times

"Everyone understands that when you move from an open outcry system to an electronic one, there is a learning curve. We've been climbing that curve quite steeply."

Pascal Samaran, CEO, MATIF

There were cynics inside and outside Paris who felt that the exchange had been caught entirely unprepared for the headlong rush into full-time screen dealing. For some weeks it looked as if the loss of credibility could do lasting damage to the exchange. Given that SBF (the French stock-market parent of MATIF) had been keen to sell the NSC system to LIFFE only weeks earlier, cynical London traders claimed that the French wanted to ensure that London was brought to its knees.

However, gradually MATIF weathered the storm and the damning indictment of the embarrassing incompetence of Salomon Brothers helped to rejuvenate confidence on the exchange. Yet at one stage there had been ominous signs of MATIF not only shooting itself in the foot, but adding to the damage by seeking to get the bullet out with a rusty pair of gangrene-inducing tweezers. MATIF found itself coming under fire for moving just a little too quickly. The Capital Market Revolution will vastly increase the need for a completely new way to handle the aftermath of error trades both within an exchange and in the broader media. Even in the information age of increasingly sophisticated technology, confidence in a market is as important now as it was in Amsterdam or London during the early sixteenth century.

Nevertheless, MATIF was at least up and running with its electronic platform after what was always bound to be a very difficult process of change-over. Although it had made mistakes, it was at least in a position to continue its aggressive promotion as it strove to make itself an essential market component in the post-EMU marketplace. Meanwhile its rivals, such as LIFFE, had yet to make the change to screen trading. In a world where exchanges had had it easy for too long, more and more evidence was accumulating that suggested a lack of management skills. MATIF had lost the ball but quickly grabbed it back. Other markets could not even make up their minds whether they had the ball or not.

What MATIF taught other markets

Pascal Samaran was ultimately proved correct when he claimed: "MATIF is the first derivative exchange in the world to move successfully from open outcry to electronic trading." But it had taken collateral damage and created a blueprint of tips for other exchanges to bear in mind. The process was certainly not as smooth as it could have been.

There were important aspects to MATIF change-over which were useful indications for exchange managements looking to change to screen trading. Firstly there was a silly *faux pas* with the systems. The VF system (for futures markets) incorporates the capacity to enter "stop" orders (orders at a predetermined level that are not triggered until the market trades through them – a popular means of containing losses in volatile futures markets). The VO for options markets did not, as such orders are less popular in options markets due to lower liquidity. But MATIF, in a process of shuffling the markets between the Paris options market (MONEP) and MATIF (futures and options on commodities and financial markets), opted to place the CAC 40 stock index futures on the VO system so they would trade side-by-side with the stock options products. The resulting lack of a stop facility was a big problem for many traders and MATIF soon switched the CAC futures on to VF to help traders place stop orders.

> The key weakness of MATIF move was to underestimate the dynamic changes of the market once it goes from open outcry to screen-based trading.

The key weakness of the MATIF move was to underestimate the dynamic changes of the market once it goes from open outcry to screen-based trading. Given that this was the first derivatives market in the world to make such a switch, MATIF did well to close up several loopholes relatively swiftly.

For a start, there was the issue of dealing with order entry problems. While MATIF can rightly claim to have installed a state-of-the-art surveillance room in its Paris headquarters, the lack of transparency in the electronic order entry process compared with open outcry means that the rules need to be amended. Indeed, the whole concept of "manifest error" is now much more difficult to discern, especially where a larger size order than claimed is entered. The problem of a large counterparty crying wolf after its attempt to shift a market fails is a big concern here. Such bullying by market counterparties threatens the credibility of the exchange. While locals and independents must understand that Darwinian survival of the fittest principles are at work in financial markets, they still enter the market in the belief it is a fair environment. Ultimately, many brokers and dealers will find themselves being punished for errors of size that they would have escaped in open-outcry scenarios. The primacy of the market will increasingly rule.

When errors occur, the market needs to have set procedures to deal with the "out trade." In the case of MATIF, allegations in the *Financial Times* on Wednesday 30 July 1998 described how "MATIF has been inconsistent in the way it has mediated trading disputes." MATIF's attempts to amend its policy while errors were still happening put it in a very tricky situation. Making policy on the hoof is a highly delicate affair in a dynamic business such as trading. Moreover, it will invariably lead to irritation as some traders see it as some form of fudge to cover up inadequacies of certain counterparties or the exchange itself.

By being first, MATIF highlighted the changes that other markets switching from open outcry to electronic markets had to make. Despite many open-outcry exchanges having spent years developing overnight markets, they were much less liquid cousins of the main market. Once the daily "big ticket" volume hit the MATIF exchange, there were different situations to be borne in mind. MATIF's pioneering move from open outcry to electronic trading was a brave move. Ultimately, it pulled it off after a few unexpected delays en route.

New-model market relations

> "I do believe that anybody should be free to shoot himself in the head provided that he doesn't hit anybody else."
>
> **Pascal Samaran, CEO, MATIF**

In error scenarios, the open-outcry markets always made counterparties (or at least the brokers acting for end users) transparently clear as their dealing was widely witnessed at first hand in the pits. With electronic trading, this is not clear. Moreover, the electronic exchanges need to rethink radically their public relations and their relationships with the media. Even in the case of an error in which the counterparties are being discussed via an electronic market, publications find themselves constrained by libel laws from naming the counterparties. The problem is that electronic markets need the maximum amount of transparency. The new era of electronic trading will not change the fact that many traders are prone to gossip, rumor, innuendo and conspiracy theories. The exchanges are merely encouraging such tittle-tattle by withholding information from the broad market. Full publicity of the counterparties to any exceptional trading scenario is required as soon as possible after an incident

Exchanges claiming confidentiality clauses merely promote a feeling that there is indeed something to hide.

occurs. The names of the counterparties ought to be available within minutes. Where they are withheld, the exchanges are only encouraging a lack of transparency. Screens were designed to be a cheaper, more convenient, faster method of dealing – they were not intended to "cloudify" what was happening. If counterparties enter a market, they must be willing to wear their errors openly and feel the heat in the immediate aftermath. Exchanges claiming confidentiality clauses merely promote a feeling that there is indeed something to hide. The cozy tradition of exchanges protecting their members' "errors" simply will not wash in the information age.

This is not merely being wise after the event. The effective management of risks of any type involves thinking the unthinkable – and catering for it. The human capacity for ingenuity means that, whatever mechanism exchanges introduce for trading, there will always be new ways for traders to lose money erroneously and endanger the sanctity of the system. Exchanges need to employ the most open architecture imaginable – in both senses of the phrase. First there is open architecture in relation to the API with which third party software vendors gain access to the exchange mechanism. The second, and just as vital, piece of open architecture is the interface with which exchanges communicate with the members, media and public alike. The former API mechanism has been much talked about in recent years. The latter interface with the end users is every bit as vital, yet exchanges continue to neglect it at their peril. Nevertheless, the need for transparency is central to the Capital Market Revolution, because of its unique capacity to transfer information as never before in history. There is no excuse for exchanges lacking transparency – in any part of their dealings. Exposing members' lapses is a necessary evil.

Meanwhile, exchanges everywhere need to instil in their members a clear idea of their responsibilities as members of the exchange. If exchanges are not prepared to suffer the consequences of their traders' actions, they should not allow the individuals concerned anywhere near a telephone, keyboard or any other communication tool. Equally, the institutions concerned ultimately ought not to be permitted membership of any legitimate exchange. Indeed, we believe that expulsion proceedings against a leading investment bank will occur by 2005, as a result of it breaching the ethics and laws of an exchange while trying to gain an unfair advantage in either derivatives or stock markets.

Alles in Ordnung – or Alice in Wonderland?

"There is no free lunch in electronic trading."

Jorg Franke, CEO, EUREX

Ironically, the first exchange to find itself suffering a substantial error in the wake of MATIF's Salomons experience was the EUREX exchange – an all-electronic market since its foundation in 1988 (as SOFFEX, the Swiss Options and Financial Futures Exchange the junior partner in the EUREX alliance). In 1998, a year when the exchange's dash for growth had finally paid off with three-figure percentage volume growth and victory in the battle for the Bund, EUREX was already suffering certain downsides from its growth. As we have already noted, the German DTB platform being used on the German-Swiss market was showing the strain.

The error of 18 November 1998 was by all accounts a monstrous one. A small German bank created a position of some 24 000 lots. As ever there was a raft of rumors and widespread inaccuracy in the media's reporting of events. The enmity between the London traders and their German counterparts in Frankfurt was quite possibly another element in the extent of the anti-EUREX rhetoric that rapidly became apparent. Nevertheless, in a situation in which – in the midst of the Capital Market Revolution – transparency was vital, the EUREX exchange comprehensively failed to grasp the mettle.

The actual events of the "error" were rather bizarre. (Although given what happens to traders all over the world on a daily basis, not so bizarre as to be truly unbelievable. Incredible maybe, but still eminently plausible.) At around 08.05 on 18 November a series of large offers suddenly appeared on users' EUREX screens. The selling frenzy continued until around 08.22. At approximately 08.44 EUREX apparently stated that all trades were valid. We do know that the actual EUREX trading mechanism worked well, facilitating trades as required.

Apparently when the offers first entered the system, EUREX market surveillance noted the order size and telephoned the bank concerned, as they were significantly larger than this small institution's normal clips. EUREX control were apparently assured everything was fine. When the offers came closer to the market, EUREX surveillance supposedly called back. Again, they were assured that everything was in order. Alas, if this was true, it was more a case of "Alice in Wonderland" than "*Alles in Ordnung*" at the bank in question. Eventually, as the market was being battered in a very disorderly fashion by the offers, something clicked either between EUREX control and the bank, or within the bank itself, and the selling abated. We believe this 17-minute selling spree lost the bank between DEM 6 and 18 million in pre-Euro money.

> With a lack of transparency on electronic terminals, exchanges must now work doubly hard to clarify misconceptions and swat rumors as fast as possible.

Admittedly, sorting out fact from fiction in such cases is never easy. Unlike in pit trading, it is not easy to discern the culprits, or the reasons for such trades. With a lack of transparency on electronic terminals, exchanges must now work doubly hard to clarify misconceptions and scotch rumors as fast as possible. Unfortunately, while initially encouraging, the reaction of the EUREX exchange was dreadful. That said, with barely one or two exceptions, few exchanges maintain the PR capacity or management inclination to deal competently with the confusion that follows in the wake of massive out-trades.

The media reporting of the 18 November events was woefully inaccurate. Many accounts gave credence to the wildest rumors, with some suggesting an error of 130 000 lots or more. The fact that this would mean that one counterparty had traded more contracts than the total volume for the session at that stage eluded several commentators.

Circumstantial evidence immediately pointed to some form of human incompetence on a grand scale. Unfortunately, the Germans, perhaps unused to the prying Anglo-Saxon media, comprehensively failed to allay any fears concerning the strength of the market's basic institutions and market services. The only certainty was that a good third-party front-end terminal could have saved the bank from this catastrophic loss.

Rumors circulated around the markets and were repeated in some areas of the media that the error arose from a trader mistakenly believing he was on the "simulated" session which provides a test market for trainees. Apparently this was not the case, although at the time the EUREX Press Office was unable to provide any evidence to confirm that there was no "sim" session scheduled for that day. Watching the EUREX Press Office flailing impotently without any evident purpose was frankly painful. The market demonstrated that despite being in the apparent forefront of the Capital Market Revolution, it had in fact learnt little of the management necessary for successful operation in the new disintermeditated environment. In the new markets it is crucial to be fleet of foot and to understand the capacity to get a message out while under flack. Alas, the exchange still could not grasp the essential information transparency vital for operation within the New Reality. The fact remains that exchange management is weak at dealing with change, crises, and any form of challenge to the status quo.

> **The fact remains that exchange management is weak at dealing with change, crises, and any form of challenge to the status quo.**

Yet in the Capital Market Revolution the status quo will remain under fire for years to come – because in the new era, there is no status quo. Change is at the heart of financial market trading and it is now the turn of exchanges to feel the heat of dealing with constant upheaval. The existing elites must reform or die. There is no third way to fumble through withholding the names of incompetent counterparties or failing to clarify what has happened on an exchange. The exchanges which cannot deal with the pressure of information transparency will end up losing business to competitors who can create a decent trading platform untainted by endless suspicions of what is happening at its core. Nobody's volumes or contracts are sacred. In the new environment, just as EUREX can steal Bund business from LIFFE, any other exchange or new participant can prise this volume from the existing leading market. Clients' loyalties to traditional local marketplaces have withered and died. The New Reality will truly be appreciated only by those who can survive.

The press offices of exchanges who wish to survive the Capital Market Revolution will have to re-engineer the process of public relations in several key areas. PR people must know and understand financial markets fully – in the case of most established exchanges their staff are barely trained in the art of disseminating a sophisticated message to the broad media or the public. As members become more geographically disparate from the exchange in the electronic age it will be even more important to liaise with them. Traders who have been made redundant by the Capital Market Revolution should be retrained to disseminate a cost-effective message to the exchange, its membership, end users, and the broader media. Ex-brokers could be ideal: the pro-activity expected of brokers the world over is precisely the skill that exchange PR offices require.

After the November 1998 error shambles, the EUREX organization began to demonstrate precisely the sort of management problems that will face many organizations throughout the Capital Market Revolution. Internal reporting appeared weak. While the direct marketing side of the exchange – which went out and sold systems or dealt with potential new members – was strong, the liaison – with the technology arms of the exchange mechanism – appeared poor. To be well positioned in the Capital Market Revolution management must be both most flexible and at its strongest where the forces of technological innovation meet market operations. This is an essential central factor to the whole process of the New Reality. The old bureaucracy is inadequate. Remember that ringing endorsement of change sounded by FIA President John Damgard: "the status quo won't do."

There were also weaknesses in the whole operation of EUREX). The syllabus for the EUREX traders' exam contains a list of about 2 400 questions from which some 144 are extracted for the exam. Amazingly, these concentrate on theoretical market and contract issues, with little emphasis on ethics training. Moreover, they test understanding electronic trading but do not address how to actually trade using EUREX screens!

The point is that management of exchanges needs to be much more closely attuned to the entire process of the dynamics of change. Whereas in the past the well-being of an exchange depended upon a strong cycle of innovation and then strong marketing to kick-start new contracts, the New Reality dictates that exchanges must see their end users as customers and treat them as such. New forms of broker–client relationship require changes in opinions about clients and shifts in client operations. To a certain degree exchanges have already done this at product development level, but in a greater globalized marketplace – with members all over the world – exchanges need to work harder at updating their client liaison function as they strive for profit status and abandon the old membership structures.

> **The New Reality dictates that exchanges must see their end users as customers and treat them as such.**

The EUREX example serves as an interesting demonstration of just how the virtuous circle of growth in an exchange may render it susceptible to substantial collateral damage in the future. When the DTB was first begun, the aim was to create an exchange in Frankfurt operating electronically to trade German products. As the dynamics of the derivatives industry accelerated, the DTB (and subsequently EUREX) progressed to spreading its screens throughout the world from Chicago through New York, London, and Frankfurt. However, as we have already mentioned, the operation of Moore's Law – which states that computer chip capacity doubles every 18 months – meant by the end of the 1980s the EUREX exchange was in a position in which the core of its system was significantly dated.

Problems with the system became increasingly frequent as it was expanded. Eventually, in late 1998, the EUREX exchange halted new terminal connections for several months in order to sort out some minor technical difficulties.[3] The German computer systems were beginning to crack under the strain of the explosive growth in EUREX trading. The system had originally been designed for 20 000 trades per day. By Q1 1999 it was having to handle an average of 58 000 daily transactions.

The EUREX system had developed perhaps the most frightening problem of all. Rather than simply falling over, spitting out unfilled orders, the system developed a marked tendency to go slow. This, for anybody who had an order in the system, was terrifying, as the system would execute the position potentially some way from the prevailing market price. Canceling the order became basically impossible. The system's bouts of sloth became so well documented that at least one regular occurrence, "the 4 p.m. problem" was officially recognized by exchange management. The risks to the trader were enormous.

As user irritation mounted, the UK Futures and Options Association (FOA) wrote to EUREX in late 1998 on behalf of 20 members who were unhappy about various aspects of the market's operation. Since the original system was ten years old, perhaps we ought to have been impressed that the EUREX machinery still worked with even a modicum of reliability, given the staggering volume growth of that year! Nevertheless, the problems of the dated EUREX technology were only too evident, especially in comparison with the French NSC system now up to speed and the LIFFE Connect system being readied for introduction within months. With several contenders seeking to be the Euro contract benchmark, the EUREX exchange faced the danger of being a short-lived leader in German Bunds with the Euro currency and technological worries threatening their market share.

The FOA letter and other system problems were discussed during a meeting between members and EUREX at Gibson Hall, London on

25 November 1998. In a relatively prickly situation, EUREX's desire to stimulate open debate was (at least perceptually) undermined by the fact that delegates had to submit any questions in writing before what Chairman (and EUREX CEO) Jorg Franke later heralded as a "very open session" had even started. To the Anglo-Saxons, raised on a degree of interminable rights to free speech, such bureaucracy smacked of totalitarianism and an incapacity to understand the client base. True, one ought to allow for translation issues, but such controlled bureaucracy reminded London traders of the failings of large behemoths such as the EU. In the information age, the demand for questions in advance seemed to underline that EUREX did not understand the dynamics of the process of electronic trading in which they had originally occupied the foreground.

Overall, EUREX had been an amazing success. Ironically, its problems stemmed directly from its successful aggressive marketing. The EUREX hardware platform and software systems were undergoing comprehensive upgrading behind the scenes in Frankfurt as the exchange urgently sought to keep abreast of the surging demand for its services.

> It is the exchanges' responsibility to clarify, clarify, clarify – not cloudify, cloudify, cloudify.

Electronic markets may have a better audit trail, but there are still questions of accessibility. And poor information flow harms credibility. Traders are only as good as the information provided. It is the exchanges' responsibility to clarify, clarify, clarify – not cloudify, cloudify, cloudify. Blanket denials without further discussion only help the rumormongers.

Electronic trading must be marketed and publicized properly. Otherwise, what occurs at the edge of the envelope (regardless of whether the exchange is 100 percent innocent or not), only makes the whole process look unreliable. Doubtless there will always be a few demented Luddites trying to undermine the game. However, if a significant crowd understand the situation, then destructive rumors are less likely to be given credence.

Part of the solution lies in a radical rethink of the way exchanges relate to the media and their membership. The market that does that will benefit itself and the whole business of electronic trading, while saving market participants from playing a lot of silly charades and expending valuable time trying to access the truth.

The Capital Market Revolution won't take any prisoners. Equally, there will not be absolute victors – at least not for many years to come. Nevertheless, there will be many absolute victims in the early years of the new millennium. Many exchanges will win battles only to find themselves suddenly besieged and cut off from essential supplies. This will be war on a massive grand scale with a significant element of attrition. Exchanges may find themselves in the lead only to suffer the humiliation of closure or being pressurized into "shotgun" mergers with competitors, some of whom have not even yet entered the fray at the time of writing.

Perhaps the richest irony of the Capital Market Revolution to-date has been the way in which despite all the technological innovation the business of strong management has if anything become even more essential. Indeed, the whole process has become a minefield for managements who were more used to the greater transparency afforded by open outcry.

Notes

1 This information is based on Patrick Young, "The New Frontiers of Risk," *Applied Derivatives Trading*, January 1999 (http://www.adtrading.com).

2 The "kerb" refers to the process of dealing with "out" trades.

3 For "minor technical problems" read "the system was old, tired, and fairly unreliable." Readers may note an ironic similarity between the behavior of the EUREX computers' reticence to function properly during the late 1990s and the antics of the German IG Metall union every time annual pay negotiations are looming.

CHAPTER 5

New management for the New Reality

Where institutions need to get it right

> "The key to winning in online brokerage is harnessing state-of-the-art execution technology to the essential analytical and sales capabilities of the best existing brokers. Even with all the advances of modern technology, people still matter."
>
> **Mike Stiller, MD, Global Direct Dealing**

While exchanges are caught right in the forefront of the new reality, institutions need to be equally aware of just how much they can gain – and indeed lose – from the whole process of Capital Market Revolution.

Managing financial institutions during the Capital Market Revolution involves huge risks, but in many ways the greatest risks will be faced by those who remain passive in the face of change. The former Premier of Northern Ireland, Brian Faulkner, once memorably remarked about the business of governing in the politically charged province during the 1960s and 1970s: "There are three things that can be done in Ulster politics, the right thing, the wrong thing, or nothing at all. I have always thought it better to do the wrong thing than nothing at all." In the Capital Market Revolution doing the "wrong" thing may well turn out to be better than merely sitting baffled by the dynamics of the process. The weak will die in the revolution while the strong will flourish. However, strength is not necessarily still defined in terms of grand scales of competence in huge institutions.

The new microbrokers

"Inevitably, some entrepreneur, whom Schumpeter dubbed the conductor, introduces an innovation so radical that it disrupts the very stability that had made it possible. The conductor sometimes makes a killing for himself, but more frequently just clears a path for others which leads to a 'swarming' of imitators. The swarm feeds on money and churns out 'progress.' People rush to feed the swarm and, in our age, the stock market rises. Banks rush to feed the swarm, and credit loosens. Old rules no longer apply. Old lessons must be unlearned, and the consequences of the innovation fully absorbed. People are forced to break with the past, to change and to make mistakes. Innovation begets more innovation as well as imitation."

Steve Zwick, *Time Magazine*

Looking out of the window from a modest second-storey tower-block office in the Wan Chai district of Hong Kong's central island, Jean-Yves Sireau does not immediately look like the head of an international stockbrokerage network that spans the globe. Yet this is precisely the softly-spoken Frenchman's role. His Mr Market organization is poised to become a genuine phenomenon of the Capital Market Revolution.

Sireau has the advantages of being a former fund manager and bank trader, coupled with a lifelong interest in computer technology. Still in his twenties, this thin bespectacled native of Paris, France, looks almost frail in comparison to the corpulent stereotype of a typical stockbrokerage boss. Yet Sireau has grasped the core elements required to run a successful financial institution in the new era. The concept is simple, the execution precise, and the organization provides a blueprint for the new-era financial institutions.

In phase one of his operations, the Mr Market software provided established stockbrokers with a chance to become part of an international network. Traditionally, stockbrokers have been parochial, dealing only with the nearest large market. Originally, this was in the nearest market town. Gradually, as the twentieth century moved on, the regional stock markets gained control (for example, in the UK there were regional markets as far afield as Belfast, Edinburgh, and the Isle of Man; the Paris Bourse united stock markets all over France). Gradually, the stock markets became unified in the capital or largest mercantile city (for example capitals such as Paris in France, London in England, Sydney in Australia. However, dealing cross-border was traditionally difficult and expensive, especially for private clients.

Access all areas

The Internet revolution sparked an explosion of interest in online dealing. Using Mr Market software, a regional or small national stockbroker can be transformed overnight into a global online stock-broking house, with the capacity to rival the largest players in the world. Moreover, a local stockbroker can now expand their vision easily beyond the narrow limits of the local bourse to look at the entire world. A stockbroker in the northern English town of Manchester can now link into the Mr Market network and access the American stock exchanges with a partner operation in New York. Similarly, a broker in Tokyo can deal directly into Bangkok, Paris, Shanghai, or anywhere in the world. The costs to the broker are minimal – a small percentage of the total brokerage goes direct to the Mr Market organization. In return, Mr Market provides an online dealing service over the Internet, using secure servers, and then reconciles all the account details, which the end client can access online in real time. All the members of the network need to do is create offset stock-clearing relationships with each other to ensure smooth settlement. In terms of cost to the original broker, there is little or no capital expenditure except for a small administrative set-up fee and a few hours training of the broker's back office staff in the reconciliation process.

Before the information revolution hit financial markets, creating a global stock brokerage from a local base was a capital-intensive operation requiring many years and millions of dollars in investment in real estate, communications, staff, and infrastructure, not to mention an adherence to local regulatory regimes wherever one established an office. Today, a global stockbrokerage can be up and running within a matter of hours. If ever there was a process to demonstrate the radical upheaval of the information age promoting the Capital Market Revolution, then Mr Market is it.

Enter the McBrokerage?

In the second phase of the Mr Market operation there is now a franchise for those who are not currently operating a stockbrokerage to enter this business. Mr Market has devised a franchise plan that can make entering the stockbrokerage business essentially as simple as opening a fast food franchise. Of course, the broker must comply with local financial regulation. Nevertheless, there is now the opportunity for the first time in history for a micro-dealing revolution. Theoretically, one person armed with a laptop can operate a global stockbrokerage from a serviced office anywhere in the world. It does not even have to be an office – it may actually be a study, or even the kitchen table, at home. And home can be anywhere in the world. This may be an extreme example but it proves just how the previous obsession with sheer bulk in financial markets is increasingly a thing of the past. Thus a tiny stockbrokerage can operate offshore while permitting its clients to access it via the Internet from whichever jurisdiction is the most benign to its requirements. With the exception of stamp duties and withholding taxes on dividends levied at source, the governments of the world will be ultimately powerless to tax investments as they flow throughout the world's stock markets. Equally, by using networks such as Mr Market, money will flow freely to the most efficient markets. In other words, economies will levy withholding taxes at their peril, as money will simply flow to the most efficient alternative. On an exchange basis, this emphasizes that the rule of the New Reality ("no one person or party's place in the trading chain is now assured") applies equally to brokers, traders, exchanges, and governments.

Of course, a great many people may feel wary about entrusting their money to such a tiny broker. In fact, with an electronic broker, the risks to the client can be utterly minimal. For a start, with the likes of Mr Market, one can use a custodian bank to take deposits of money and hold the money in escrow against stock dealings. When a trade is executed, the client's account (with a leading global custodian bank such as Bank of Bermuda) is debited the cost of the shares while the global custody arm of the bank holds the shares in a nominee account for the purchaser. In other words, the account can be established so that no money actually flows directly through the broker's office at all. The predetermined

> **Even the humblest retail clients can now establish themselves as global stock traders from a single account.**

commission is merely credited to the broker's account after every transaction. So the broker never actually gets to touch your money but you can have access to a confidential global stockbrokerage while your money remains on deposit with a top-rated custodian bank which also holds all your share certificates in electronic form (as has become the norm on stock markets these days). When you enter an order to deal, the computer first checks your account to ensure you have sufficient funds to buy the shares. Once this has been cleared, the orders can be executed online within seconds to any exchange in the world. Even the humblest retail clients can now establish themselves as global stock traders from a single account. This is a facility that even the large online brokers such as Schwab and E-Trade have yet to establish at the time of writing. However, given the explosive growth in their domestic businesses, this is hardly surprising. We will be examining further the amazing rise of online trading in a later chapter.

A global online securities trading business is now at the fingertips of those who are sufficiently nimble to capitalize on the market. The largest investment banks will remain in hugely expensive CBD offices with branches all over the world, cranking out megadeals as they have done for years. Indeed, the wave of merger mania will continue throughout the global banking industry until probably only a few dozen Titans are left. However, they will find themselves having to play against significant niche competition which can use the dynamics of the New Reality and the flexibility of information technology to its advantage.

In the Capital Market Revolution the virtual securities house is a reality. Nowadays, investment banks have to employ a vast array of specialists in all parts of the globe to be assured of securing suitable capacity when deals arise. This overhead-intensive situation means that turnover must be high, since without a constant flow-through of deals, the overheads cripple the banks' profitability. Return on capital is the mantra of the banking industry, wholesale and retail. In the Capital Market Revolution the combination of nimbleness and much lower capital requirements hands the advantage in many lines of work straight to the "microbankers."

Finding your global niche

In the September–October 1998 *Harvard Business Review* researcher Robert Laubacher and Thomas W. Malone, a Professor of Information Technology systems at MIT, contributed an intriguing paper entitled "The Dawn of the E-Lance Economy". The article discussed the development of Linux, a new computer development system that was created by Linus Torvalds, a University of Helsinki student. The system was developed online by a vast number of programmers in a form of co-operative effort, as a sort of peer group bug-fix and upgrade. As the paper noted:

> What the Linux story really shows us is the power of a new technology –
> in this case, electronic networks – to fundamentally change the way work
> is done. The Linux community, a temporary, self-managed gathering of

diverse individuals engaged in a common task, is a model for a new kind of business organization that could form the basis for a new kind of economy ... And in some industries, like investment banking and consulting, it is often easier to understand the existing organizations not as traditional hierarchies but as confederations of entrepreneurs, united only by a common brand name.

The problem for the networks of entrepreneurs within the investment banking business today is that their own networks are hugely bureaucratic and relatively slow-moving, thanks to pressures of regulation and the sheer size of their operations. The

> **During and after the Capital Market Revolution, the rewards will go to the most flexible, lateral thinking (and operating) entities.**

fact is that a smaller network, perhaps one that recomposes itself at regular intervals, can threaten to remove a lot of the megabanks' profitability.

As Laubacher and Malone note:

> Business organizations are, in essence, mechanisms for co-ordination. They exist to guide the flow of work, materials, ideas, and money, and the form they take is strongly affected by the co-ordination technologies available. Until a hundred years or so ago, co-ordination technologies were primitive.

During and after the Capital Market Revolution, the rewards will go to the most flexible, lateral thinking (and operating) entities. The problem with current megabanks is that, by their very definition, they often find themselves constrained from acting in their clients' best interests, either because the client cannot react in time, or more frequently because the megabank itself is incapable of offering innovative flexible solutions within a sufficiently brief space of time.

So, in the New Reality, Laubacher and Malone are correct when they identify that:

> In one sense, the new co-ordination technologies enable us to return to the preindustrial organizational model of tiny, autonomous businesses – businesses of one or of a few – conducting transactions with one another in a market. But there's one crucial difference: electronic networks enable

these microbusinesses to tap into the global reservoirs of information, expertise, and financing that used to be available only to large companies. The small companies enjoy many of the benefits of the big without sacrificing the leanness, flexibility, and creativity of the small.

The megabanks will continue to do the largest deals, but the microbankers will only require mere crusts from the table to produce infinitely better returns on capital in the new era. In fact, the microbankers will be able to take on deals vastly beyond their proportionate resources compared to the megabanks. Equally, the microbankers will not have the same exposure to potentially crippling losses caused by management inefficiency which have all too often blighted the banking industry throughout history. Until the twentieth century, the great bankers had often been small family-owned units with a degree of mercantile orientation that astounded the world. In the contemporary era the megabanks will still proliferate at the global level but – at the same time – for those not running multinational organizations the key to future success will lie with a new grouping of microbankers. These microbankers will be able to operate in any market, and will have the added advantage of not being tied to a particular marketplace.

The DPO threatens the exchange

Direct Public Offering (DPO) is a route that was initially used by Andrew Klein's Spring Street Brewery to go direct to the public to sell stock. Using the Internet was a critical part of his approach. Other famous DPO structures in the USA in previous years had included Ben and Jerrys' boutique ice-cream operation offering stocks for sale on the tubs of their product. In Klein's case, the Internet was only one part of his stock-selling operation, which also included product packaging on his beer cans. However, it was the part that inadvertently started his move to become the Internet's first investment banker.

Interestingly, Klein actually started Wit Capital as an online investment bank selling stock because he perceived investors still felt exchanges had a certain degree of integrity that they could not guarantee through a direct offering. Post-issue trading was also far superior than that offered even on the pioneering billboard produced by Spring Street some months after its DPO. However, we believe that in the longer term, perhaps through using a clearing house, an online stock market or online stock issuer will find considerable success through using the DPO process to help revolutionize the venture capital business, and with it create a credible alternative, at least for small traded stocks.

Moreover, we see the entire nature of stock issuance changing. For instance, in a marketplace where smaller issues are economic, why must large institutions be the only underwriters? We believe that in the near future not merely microbrokers but large high-net-worth individual traders will be able to participate in the underwriting process. This will be a genuine revolution in financial markets, since existing underwriters are used to extorting something

> **The infusion of more underwriters can only help create more equity issues and help reduce the costs to corporations of coming to market.**

little short of monopoly rent for their moderate risk-taking activity in the issuance of shares. The infusion of more underwriters can only help create more equity issues and help reduce the costs to corporations of coming to market. Indeed, in the late nineteenth and early twentieth centuries, as Ron Chernow noted in *The Death of the Banker,* "wealthy individuals often participated as underwriters in large securities offerings, an arrangement that pointed up both the paucity of capital and the limited distribution network of investment houses, which didn't have thousands of brokers ready to stuff stocks and bonds into the accounts of pliant small investors."

Down but not out

"Technology has dramatically reduced the cost of executing a trade. Suddenly, broker expertise might not be as valuable as brokers want investors to believe."

Andrew Klein, founder, Wit Capital Corporation

Existing companies still carry a considerable advantage over the new operators entering a market. Their established reputations, quality brand names, and ongoing relationships with clients count for a lot. Even in the front line of the Capital Market Revolution they can still prosper. However, they will have to shed a great many of their underlying precepts and old methods of dealing. Management will need to be able to think laterally. Companies will also have to lose a vast number of staff, to fit in with the new microbanking ethos. Thinking the unthinkable will in many ways be the only way for existing companies to avoid becoming victims of the Capital Market Revolution.

Take brokerage for instance. It really does not matter what product we look at in terms of the product line. Stocks, commodities, any form of exchange derivative product – the end result is likely to be very similar. For example, in the old days of futures dealing the fastest way of working was if different staff stood at various parts of a dealing desk and shouted out prices to the brokers around them. When a broker gave an order, it was shouted to a "link" person who passed it from the office down the telephone line to the floor broker who signaled the order into the pit. Remarkably, this could all be done in a split second. Meanwhile, in the stockmarket, it became commonplace to have a desk of "dealers" who did not speak directly to clients but executed orders for the brokers, who in turn rang the dealers with the orders or walked over to their desks with them. Again, this was a cumbersome process.

As screen-based exchanges have proliferated and new front ends have been added to the screens, which make the markets more accessible and easier to trade, many brokers have shown a marked reluctance to escape from the constraints of their old dealing processes. For all their claims of floors being inefficient, many institutional managements are still happy to add to the bureaucracy of tickets and orders already stifling dealing desks on a busy day. For instance, there are those who keep "throttling" their business at a variety of standpoints. The term "throttling" is used in financial software parlance as a term to describe any bottleneck that is created by the client's reluctance to adapt new technology to the best of its abilities. So, for example, when screens have been introduced to many dealing areas, there have been many institutions which merely retrained their link people and placed them on or beside the computer terminals. So, the brokers had to shout at the "links" to enter their orders into the computer terminals. This is such an archaic process as to be truly moronic.

When front-end terminals can route orders to dozens of different contracts (or stocks, or indeed a mixture of financial

> **In the modern era the days of shouting at link people are over.**

products), why is there not a terminal on every broker's desk? Many investment banks have a desire to swamp their brokers with passive information screens, such as Reuters or Telerate, or marginally interactive ones such as Bloomberg, yet they resolutely refuse to give their traders direct access to the market. Instead, brokers are expected to place their orders via an intermediary within the room (such as a link person) who enters an order on to the computer screen in question. Meanwhile, the broker must usually produce a handwritten and time-stamped order-entry ticket (to create audit trail) while simultaneously entering the order into an electronic back-office system. If the brokers are already entering the order into an electronic order system, then why can they not place that order directly into the marketplace? It sounds foolish, yet it remains company policy at many leading brokerage houses.

Such a process is not merely bureaucratic and vastly labor-intensive (and with CBD rents and rates to be paid, overhead-intensive). Equally, it prevents the broker from being fully autonomous. In the modern era the days of shouting at link people are over. In the Capital Market Revolution disintermediation affects not just external broker/client/exchange relationships but also every single internal management and dealing process. Those who maintain artificial barriers to direct trade within their organizations will find themselves out of business, along with those exchanges which cannot understand the New Reality. Indeed, the modern era will see a drastic reduction in the number of brokers required. This is because electronic access systems now incorporate simple risk-management functions, and have the capacity to deal faster than human co-ordination can manage,

The stock market brokers have been bloated by boom.

therefore the whole broker's role is under threat. So, the New Reality impinges on the micro level – i.e. every individual broker in the food chain – just as much as it will impact large institutions and even governments.

As the Capital Markets Revolution gains momentum, the hordes of employed brokers will find their numbers drastically reduced. Indeed, with the growing merger mania amongst existing banks this has already been a shrinking workforce during the past decade, despite a raft of new products in the derivatives arena. The stock market brokers have been bloated by boom. Even before stock market prices take a downturn or volume dwindles, the ranks of brokers are in for a big shakeout.

The NewVas paradigm

"Financial Services firms are not good at coping with rapid change."
The Economist

In the new era, brokers are going to need to be smarter, more conversant with product areas outside their own horizons, and have a greater global knowledge than ever before. With a diversified client base, linguistic skills will remain at a premium. English is undoubtedly the global language of financial markets – a trend that will continue unabated in the new millennium. However, clients like being spoken to in their own language. As the broker's job becomes less that of an order gatherer and more of a dynamic client liaison person, the person who can speak to customers in their domestic language will be highly valued. The successful broker in the new millennium will have to be capable of providing "New Value Added Services" ("NewVas"). NewVas will include being more in touch with every aspect of a client's business. The old days of a broker who merely regurgitated a few lines of research and then spent the day shouting orders into markets at a clients' behest while providing heavily price-driven information, are already over. NewVas brokers will no longer have a handful of clients to deal with. Rather they will have already handed over screens to several dozen clients who will enter their orders directly to the market through the brokerage company's own screens. In many respects, the broker's job will now become one akin to a trainer or coach. They will need to create a great deal of their own analysis to give clients an edge in the market. The NewVas brokers will be well read, with a vast under-standing of the markets, as well as more traditional broker "savvy." The old style "wide-boys" which London's East End exported to the world are going to face extinction unless they can learn a great deal more about how and why markets function on both a micro and macro level. Their role as glorified trade processors will not last beyond the next five years.

NewVas brokers will utilize a range of technological methods to commuicate with clients. Obviously, speaking daily to their clients will be only one of them. Client visits and other regular facilities are already becoming established practices at many blue-chip operations – although they remain remarkably scarce at some leading brokerages the authors could mention. In fact, the sheer incapacity of some brokerages to understand what the information revolution is all about is truly frightening. A supposedly technologically-oriented London brokerage moved into high-tech new premises in 1998, complete with state-of-the-art flat screens, etc., only for their dealers to be told a few months later that they were to be prevented from adding any attachments to e-mails, in order to save on bandwidth charges! Unfortunately, management this far out of touch with reality will increase in the next few years. However, as the Capital Market Revolution accelerates, such Luddite companies, bereft of even a grain of comprehension about the future of financial markets, will become extinct. Ironically, instead of paying more for bandwidth, the same company promptly decided to invest considerable amounts of staff time and a portion of the software budget on monitoring all incoming and outgoing e-mail to ensure it was politically correct and in accordance with guidelines from its banking parent. This sort of double whammy makes us confident this brokerage will not survive much beyond the dawn of the new millennium without radical upheaval. In fact, the brokerage in question closed during the first quarter of 1999, even before this book was published.

More bottlenecks

Another major area of throttling will occur where the old management of dealing rooms fail to take account of the technological requirements of their operations. Throttling through inadequate bandwidth will be a common sight in the early years of the new millennium, as managements strain to keep their fixed costs down – while not understanding what they require from their technological capability.

Indeed, in the whole area of technology many banks are very poorly positioned. In the New Reality managers who can understand IT will start at a significant advantage to their competition. Similarly, the IT management who can understand the business of broking, dealing, and investment banking as a whole without feeling insecure or irritated at how the "masters of the universe" receive often stratospheric rewards will prosper. Indeed, the senior management of investment banks who foster computer literacy in their dealing management, as well as dealing literacy in their computer management, have already reaped significant rewards during the past ten years. As the information revolution continues to

> **Those who are insufficiently technologically literate will wither away and die.**

gather pace in financial markets, so the process of managing any investment banking operation will increasingly pivot around the maximum exploitation of technology. Just about every aspect of modern financial markets can now be commoditized/productized and in some way rendered an automated/electronic process – so encouraging a lower-margin, higher-volume business. This can only help to trim staff numbers and also lead to downward pressures on brokerage, and income for clients and brokers in all but the most esoteric areas of financial markets. Those who are insufficiently technologically literate will wither away and die. Depending on how much of their capital resources they wish to waste, it will only be a matter of time.

Discounted broker – but not discount brokers

There is one enormous misconception that existing brokers have about the process of brokerages going online. Many "full-service" brokerages erroneously (if not contemptuously) lump online trading firms together with traditional "no frills" discount brokerage operations. In fact, the two are entirely separate. Discount brokers are providing a cheap service without any added extras. In contrast, online brokerages are merely exploiting the new technology of the Capital Market Revolution to offer a potentially huge scope of analysis, data, research, and brokerage quotes/prices, and ultimately direct market-trading access which no full service broker can ever hope to provide via one broker. Through a computer terminal (whether by direct access or via the Internet) any trader can now essentially trade the entire world of financial markets at a negligible fixed cost to their brokers. As the Capital Market Revolution gains momentum and online brokerages offer more and better extra services, the full service brokers will be annihilated. As we discuss in Chapter 6, this entire process will encourage more and more traders to become managers of their own capital, superannuation accounts, and so forth, at the expense of the current leviathan pension funds and asset managers who intermediate the process. For full service brokers, there is simply no place to hide from the Capital Market Revolution. The future of broking, like the future of trading, is online.

The new model trader

Amongst the many dealers in the world who are employing new technology, there is no single prototype for a trader. Patrick Young can now trade from his hilltop retreat in Italy, near Monaco, as if he were at the heart of the London markets he used to work in. Similarly, former floor traders from the biggest exchanges in London, Chicago, and New York are now trading from throughout the world, some in cities, some in utterly rural locations, far from the CBDs in which they once traded.

Riccardo Ronco still trades from the core of the European capital market – London. However, his methods and approach are entirely dependent upon information technology. A well-known speaker on the international trading conference circuit, Ronco has worked for several leading banks, including Crédit Agricole, Banco Ambrosiano Veneto, and latterly Banca Nazionale Dell'Agricoltura. He lives in London near to Tower Bridge, a short walk from his office in the City of London financial district, and devotes almost his entire life to researching new trading methods for financial markets. His London apartment alone houses more than 300 books devoted to trading methods.

Ronco's fascination with financial markets stems from his first encounter with a price chart of financial markets when he was researching math and physics in 1989. Fascinated by what he saw, Ronco set about using new technology to create profitable computer models. While Ronco is coy about his precise methodology, at the core of his techniques is a state matrix approach that employs directionality and volatility to describe the phase in which the system operates and to which Ronco then applies adaptive tools.

Not every trader in the Capital Market Revolution employs such technological methods. However, contemporary processor technology permits traders like Riccardo Ronco to utilize methodologies that are created from the sort of complex mathematics that were impossible to calculate in real-time until the end of the twentieth century.

In terms of the future of markets, Ronco reckons "the electronic era will surpass every method of trading, increasing the speed of markets and market volatility. There will be a lot of funds rapidly switching between markets, creating wide and wild movements, and there will be a lot of private investors (basically on the futures side) that will try to survive these waves."

Surviving screens: a trader's primer

Taking a step back from the big picture for a moment, let's examine the whole issue of how screens need to be managed in the new era. In the last chapter, we discussed the new frontiers of risk. Despite some humorous incidents, the conclusions are deadly serious. Management needs to give considerable thought to how to manage live trading screens in the dealing rooms. Such screens will continue to proliferate for several years to come and the more screens that are live, the more the risks will expand, perhaps as a geometric function. Here are a few points to ponder:

- For years, many institutions have operated with cluttered desks and kept each individual trader's personal area to a minimum. There is a good reason for this policy to be reversed in the new era. The more space brokers have, the less likely it is that an injudicious shuffling of paperwork will result in an erroneous trade on the dealing screen on their desks.
- Live screens ought to be differentiated. Color-coding of keyboards, so that the one that permits order entry is a suitably bright color, e.g. red, may be a simple and cost-effective way to ensure that the possibility of keyboard errors is reduced. The same goes for the computer mouse, which ought to be similarly color-

co-ordinated if it connects to a live screen. Management should also consider making the same screen in every dealer's bank of monitors the one devoted to live dealing. At least then all traders in an organization will know where they ought to be looking, no matter which position they are sitting at!

- Screen locks should to be applied to live-dealing terminals when they are switched off. If locks are required, key access ought to be restricted to the dealer, the IT director, and the desk manager.

- It may be wise not merely to encase screens in plastic to prevent as much danger from fluid spillage as possible, but also to ban food in trading areas. After all, everything barring small candy bars were banned from many exchange floors. Since dealers should take mandated breaks from their screens to protect their eyes from risk of damage, surely then they can eat and consume liquids away from the screens, thus reducing eye strain and also the risk of spillage on screens. Admittedly, this will disappoint desk managers in many companies who would gladly shackle their brokers to their desks if only workplace laws permitted them. However, with a bit of luck such people will be sufficiently computer-illiterate to have lost their jobs in the new millennium, so giving way to some more mature management in most dealing rooms.

> In the New Reality many banks and institutions will increasingly question whether they actually need large dealing rooms at all.

- Management must never move screens without first consulting brokers. It sounds silly, but it will happen sooner or later, with catastrophic results for some institution.

- Management must endeavor to reduce clutter on traders' desks. Removing endless paper-based memos on nebulous subjects would help keep more trees alive and leave brokers' desks a great deal less cluttered. The rule is quite simply: if it isn't of importance to trading financial markets, then don't send it to your brokers/dealers.

- Data overload is not actually healthy for traders. This may come as a surprise to management. Can between six and nine separate screens on a desk really be good for a trader, as some investment banks apparently believe? Getting rid of one or two might just improve both top-line costs and bottom-line profits, and by using execution terminals such as PATS one can trade essentially any market in the world using a single screen.

In the New Reality many banks and institutions will increasingly question whether they actually need large dealing rooms at all. Certainly a degree of information flow in such offices can be very beneficial. However, with remote dealership now a distinct possibility, we expect to see many more institutions allowing their traders to work from home. This will of course have extensive lifestyle implications for many traders who will no longer need to live within large financial districts. City dealing rooms may become mere shadows of their former selves with only the risk managers, monitoring their dealers' positions in real time, left in what was formerly a thriving dealing room. Indeed, the risk managers may themselves move to a remote location, along with other key bank support personnel. The risk management staff and the integrity/safety of the computer system will be paramount.

A further implication of a potential migration of city dealers to the countryside will be a large deflationary effect upon CBD property prices in many locations. Moreover, it will give regulators considerable headaches, as dealers may be nominally registered at a London bank but actually living in Ireland, France, or Spain. For regulators and governments, reliant on their captive monopoly powers to tax and regulate, the Capital Market Revolution will significantly erode their powers on every plain. Overall, the Capital Market Revolution will take more power from institutions and hand more power to the individual and microdealers than any other market upheaval in history. The rise to primacy of the individual is simply irresistible under the Capital Market Revolution.

CHAPTER 6

Power to the people

The staggering rise of the private individual

"As technology empowers individuals, it creates greater opportunities for us all. The marketplace will become even more efficient because of the availability of timely, uncensored information. That will almost certainly put the bureaucracies – both in government and in commerce – out of business … In the Global Paradox – the larger the world's economy, the more powerful its smallest players – it is virtually impossible to overestimate the role of global telecommunications."

John Naisbitt, *Global Paradox*

The Global Paradox hits financial markets

John Naisbitt, the noted pundit and author of books such as *MegaTrends* (which has sold in excess of eight million copies), understands perfectly the dynamics of how what he called the "Global Paradox" (the larger the world's economy, the more powerful its smallest players) will affect financial markets.

Since the Wall Street crash of 1929, and indeed before it, the world's investment markets have increasingly become the playthings of large institutionalized organizations managing billions of dollars. Such leviathans of financial management will find their territory increasingly coming under threat from the New Reality. The problem with large funds is that while big may be beautiful in terms of economies of scale, the ultimate returns tend to be relatively poor. Nowadays, backed up by an array of academic economists, defeatism reigns in many areas of money management. Many funds only aim to attain a performance close to the average and few wish to beat the index.

Those Confounded Online Traders

"Leave your job, log on and – hey presto! – you too can turn into the newest pariah of America's stockmarkets, an electronic day trader. In the 1980s, it was Wall Street's take-over barbarians. Today it is the amateurs in jeans and sneakers who sit in front of a computer and trade 40–50 times in a day. Just as they did with Gordon Gecko types in the 1980s, Wall Street's great and good are demonising day traders, accusing them of distorting the stock-market and causing volatility in share prices."

The Economist

It was clear that online trading had truly arrived when even the rather staid New York Stock Exchange wanted to change its hours to accommodate the online traders by opening as late as 10 pm in the evening. The move had been promoted by the preponderance of rival "after hours" stock trading systems, such as those created by Ashton Technology Group, which were only a regulatory step or two away from being fully fledged exchanges in their own right.

Nevertheless, the NYSE remained a fairly reactionary place in the latter months of the twentieth century. The new breed of independent day traders are simply demonstrating that now the playing field has been remodeled to permit individual traders as much access as the large corporations who traditionally dominated stock dealing. Unfortunately, the new independent traders can manage to demonstrate that some existing professional traders have been profiting merely through who they know rather than through any particular market skills on their part.

"Now that discount brokerages and the internet have opened up trading to the littlest guy, three distinct classes of day-trading society have evolved; the at home Internet cowboys, the ex-Wall Street pros, and the players who work out of day trading firms. Each group uses different strategies and different financial and electronic tools."

Carol Vinzant, *Fortune*, 15 February 1999.

The new e-local and other online traders are evidence of a new stockmarket democracy at work. If market makers can't keep their prices up-to-date with the market, then the e-traders will strike mercilessly. This is merely mass arbitrage and will ensure that only the fittest traders can survive. For too long market makers have often formed cosy cartels. Now market makers must truly demonstrate their ability to trade as well as their peers'. The fact that many may be private clients, from well-beyond the boundaries of the local financial district, only serves to add insult to injury for those proud market makers who have long sniped at the abilities of retail traders. When they meet head-to-head in the forefront of the Capital Market Revolution, many professional market makers have already been embarrassed.

Meanwhile, through enhanced liquidity, day traders make the stock market better for all investors. They have also helped press brokerage changes down to more reasonable levels in the electronic age. Their capacity to keep market makers on their toes also ensures that prices are more transparent and up-to-date throughout the trading day – a welcome boon for all those who have suffered from market makers becoming irritable at merely being asked for prices several times a day while seeking to trade. Similarly, day traders tend to be attracted to stocks or markets which are already volatile. Even financial academia agrees that online traders don't actually inflate volatility *per se.*

True, many day traders may not survive the US and European stock markets' next bear market – which will probably occur earlier in the next millennium than many traders would tend to think. However, even then a great many traders will continue to prosper, demonstrating a full range of trading skills across all types of market conditions. As *The Economist* noted in May 1999,

> "Indeed, with their expertise at trading fast and often, when the conflagration comes [day traders] may prove fleeter of foot than the big, staid institutional investors who have often been bad-mouthing them."

The new breed of day traders are here to stay. The sooner the stockmarket establishment realizes that fact, the sooner they can get on with addressing the issues within the Capital Market Revolution which threaten their very existence. Indeed, it would serve the stockmarket establishment much better to identify just how much benefit the new e-traders bring to capital markets. Just like the e-traders in the vanguard of the revolution, many large institutions will not survive unless they begin to understand the big picture of dynamic change affecting all markets. Investors large and small now face many of the same difficulties. However, it may take them some time to realize and even acknowledge that they are ostensibly in the same boat.

Modern mass-market fund management operations are often conservative, bureaucratic, and vastly overstaffed. The leviathans of funds management have become huge organizations that cannot move their holdings without affecting the underpinnings of the very markets in which they are operating. The stock markets of the world have long lacked liquidity compared to their futures market cousins. Yet the big fund managers see being able to deal by stealth as one of the few advantages they have in existing financial markets. If such a lack of transparency acts as an advantage, one is inclined to wonder why fund managers cannot make superior returns. Such a query is fully justified, for there are other more contemporary fund managers who have demonstrated remarkable returns in recent times. As the Capital Market Revolution accelerates, lumbering resource-intensive fund management organizations will increasingly resemble dinosaurs. In most cases, they will become as extinct as dinosaurs too.

> As the Capital Market Revolution accelerates, lumbering resource-intensive fund management organizations will increasingly resemble dinosaurs.

The hedge-fund phenomenon

The father of the hedge fund, Alfred Winslow Jones, was born in Australia to an American family and lived a varied life with a spell in the Berlin US Embassy as a Vice-Consul during the 1930s, having previously been a purser on a steam ship. Along the way he gained a Ph.D. in sociology, before becoming an associate editor of *Fortune Magazine*. It was on his fifth separate career, when 48 years old, that Jones created the first hedge fund with an embryonic structure that balanced:

Market exposure = (long exposure – short exposure) / capital(1)[1]

This original idea of "hedge funds" referring to funds that buy and sell equal quantities of different stock so as to remain essentially market-neutral, has now largely been abandoned by the largest players. The hedge fund of today is generally a limited partner structure based in an offshore tax haven, which can employ gearing to maximize returns. Hedge funds tend to have two key advantages over contemporary funds. Firstly, hedge funds are fast and nimble operations. They often turn around their positions swiftly and avoid illiquid markets where they might have difficulty exiting when required. Secondly, hedge funds are much more aggressive than the conventional fund managers. Hedge fund managers usually hold substantial stakes in their own funds. Such a self-interest motive, fueled by fees being linked to profits, makes the hedge fund managers much less reticent about trying to outperform whatever benchmark investors throw at them.

> The original and continuing justification for incentive fees in hedge funds is the inherent promise of superior performance – not average performance, not absolute performance, but superior performance. Prudence dictates that investors fundamentally grasp Jones's motivational dynamics and seek to replicate them in the hedge funds they choose."
>
> **William J. Crerend, Chairman, Evaluation Associates**[2]

Admittedly, some hedge funds do have their risks and investors need to always bear the *"caveat emptor"* motto in mind. Equally, hedge funds tend to be more volatile than their conventional brethren. However, while they suffer greater drawdowns (troughs from highs to lows), over the years hedge funds have proved that they can and do regularly bounce back from their periods of famine into renewed and exceptional periods of feast.

Hedge funds are now so firmly established as to be here to stay in exalted permanence: one of the holy trinity of big-league financiers, along with the world's great proprietary traders and the most leveraged of the mergers and acquisitions experts.

Hedge funds are the glamorous side of the funds management industry. Anybody arriving at a cocktail party who announces that they are a "hedge fund manager" cannot be regarded as anything but rich. After all, hedge-fund managers are those ultra-sophisticated practitioners of high finance. For them, controling a fund about three times the GDP of a small African potentate is about as simple as ordering a bagel for breakfast to the rest of us. Hedge funds are now so firmly established as to be here to stay in exalted permanence: one of the holy trinity of big-league financiers, along with the world's great proprietary traders and the most leveraged of the mergers and acquisitions experts.

New maths, new risks: the foibles of avarice

> "The fact of the matter is that there are brainy people and superb corporations throughout the world. There is no shortage of fools and suckers either."
>
> **Professor Robert Sobel**

There are of course some hedge funds that will fly Icarus-like too close to the sun and find the burnt wax on their wings causes their feathers to fall off, leading to a sickening plunge back to earth. However, overall returns in general stock-market funds tend to be pale facsimiles of the results achieved by most hedge funds.

Long Term Capital Management (LTCM) was in many ways a fairy-story example of a hedge fund. Its principals all had extensive financial backgrounds. The senior partner was John Merriwether, a former chief dealer at Salomons, and amongst the remaining partners were no less than two Nobel laureates, Myron Scholes and Robert Merton, plus a former US Federal Reserve Vice-Chairman, David Mullins. The fund raised a staggering 1.25 billion US dollars when launched in 1994 – then a new fund record. The minimum stake was 10 million dollars.

In late 1998 LTCM suffered the humiliation of being bailed out by a syndicate of banks organized by the US central bank, the Federal Reserve. LTCM had fallen apart at the seams with losses of virtually all its capital. In many ways this looked like a classic example of high finance squeezing extra returns from the mathematics of rocket science. While the collapse of LTCM is precisely an example of the foibles of the Capital Market Revolution at work, in fact the reasons for LTCM's collapse were much more the result of the age-old problem of greed over-stretching itself. Investors in hedge funds employing gearing (the vast majority) need to realize that, just as gearing can be terrific when conditions are propitious, the fall-out from losses arrives a great deal faster. Hence the problems of over-gearing with inaccurate risk management. There is a limit to the point where gearing becomes useful. Once this level is passed, the added gearing endangers the fund's well-being with remarkable alacrity. In the case of LTCM, gearing often reached staggering levels of 50 times capital or more. At these sorts of levels, the slightest bump in the carpet can send a whole fund careering into oblivion.

There is a limit to the point where gearing becomes useful.

When a consortium of banks launched a bail-out, the *Financial Times* noted that Merriwether's fund was "using a system so complex and erudite that it was thought that nothing could possibly go wrong". In other words, LTCM was the unsinkable investment, the "*Titanic*" of hedge funds. The foibles of avarice had resulted in the management forgetting a simple precept of trading. Risk management involves thinking the unthinkable. Many market observers were wont to repeat the old hedge-fund maxim: "You don't know who is swimming naked until the tide goes out."

To discuss all the aspects of the LTCM management's failings falls largely outside the scope of this volume. However, Patrick Young's initial synopsis at the time somewhat perversely identifies the nub of this hedge fund's failings: "LTCM's mathematics were impeccable. Irritatingly, the real world was for once demonstrating a fleeting flaw in its own modeling which didn't self-adjust in time to save the hedge fund from disaster."[3]

The fact is that, for all the precision of mathematics, the world retains certain minuscule imperfections. The increasingly mathematically-oriented fund managers amongst the hedge-fund ranks must understand that, even as the Capital Market Revolution reaches fruition and the new playing field is functioning smoothly, the dangers of human arrogance over the elements will remain the greatest risk to investment losses. Risk management is the most important aspect of any form of trading. Indeed, many of the best alternative fund managers often utilize fairly mundane order-entry procedures but expend huge amounts of research resources on attaining the best exit points from all trades, both loss-making and profitable.

New alternatives

The Commodity Trading Advisor (CTA) has been very much a phenomenon of the last few years. Such advisors are frequently small (often just one- or two-person) businesses, trading primarily exchange-traded derivatives. Clustered together with hedge funds, CTAs are some of the most exciting new fund managers around. The whole CTA business, allied with hedge funds, is creating an enormous new industry of specialist fund managers grounded in the most volatile markets on Earth. These will add significant advantages to returns when a judicious degree of money is invested, providing a fillip to the conventional fund-management industry.

> "It is a global shift from the state to the importance of the individual, and riding on the wave of the telecommunications revolution, the opportunities for individual freedom and enterprise are totally unprecedented."
>
> **John Naisbitt, *Global Paradox***

But do we really need conventional funds? Actually, this question can be answered with an emphatic yes and no. The existing large, sprawling CBD-based, bureaucracies will increasingly lose ground to a wide-ranging array of cyberfund managers operating off much lower cost bases with fewer staff, cheaper overheads, and all the advantages of less regulation and tax-free location that offshore status provides. The only remaining large-fund managers will be some national-oriented superannuation funds, investing

Cyberbusiness and cyberfinanciers will be able to migrate with little effort to the regime that gives them maximum flexibility.

the pension funds for those employees who find themselves still trapped under the influence of an over-intrusive government that has failed to grasp the New Reality. Government influence over all areas of life is already being significantly weakened in the electronic age, but even those governments paying lip service to the New Reality will maintain a degree of control over physical assets within their boundaries. Thus, pension funds saddled with large quantities of property will find it more difficult to move seamlessly offshore, unlike their hedge-fund and alternative-investment cousins. Any government tampering with superannuation funds will only encourage faster offshore movement but also cause their wider economy to hemorrhage. Cyberbusiness and cyberfinanciers will be able to migrate with little effort to the regime that gives them maximum flexibility. Individuals will also find more incentive (and will be more able) to move assets offshore as the power of government to trade transactions declines.

The new-model fund manager

"The investment management industry will be increasingly polarized between the whales and the goldfish. The big investment management firms will become increasingly cumbersome, converging on passive investment strategies while more talented managers split off to set up more nimbler entrepreneurial structures."

Paul Marshall of Marshall Wace Asset Management Ltd.,
quoted in *Investing With the Hedge Fund Giants* by Beverly Chandler

Conventional methods of fund management will of course still exist. However, they will exist increasingly in cyber form. By the time the Capital Market Revolution has reached its zenith, investors (regardless of jurisdiction, regardless of investment aims) will be able to click on to a Web site and select a model balance for their portfolio in seconds. The core of a portfolio for most investors will probably be simple index-tracker funds. Such funds are designed to follow market indices precisely, while some variants can also lock in profits, using derivatives, as they are accumulated at various points (say every 20 percent), regardless of whether the market subsequently drops back. Such funds can increasingly be automated. The old-style fund manager, with the emphasis on large numbers of employees, will find their margins evaporating as cheaper online alternatives grow. Such index trackers will increasingly become automated.

In the cyber age, payment on results is also likely to become more common. The old-established ways of fund managers taking large chunks of money both up-front as an entry fee and then significant fees for management, regardless of returns, will be wiped away. As we will discuss further in the next chapter, the Capital Market Revolution and indeed the dawning of the information age are all examples of the "new meritocracy." A huge upside to the information age is to give all hues of investor better, cheaper, faster access to any financial market and financial market data.

In addition to simple index trackers, future fund-management clients will have the capacity to skew their investment returns according to their preferences. Therefore, a simple index-tracker basket may be skewed to a particular national market, or have a slightly higher weighting assigned to a sector of the market (local, national, regional, or global) all at the

> **The increasing commoditization of financial products means that in future investment alternatives will be extensive.**

click of a mouse. Then clients will be able to decide in which additional funds they wish to invest the remainder of their funds. Here there will be a panoply of alternatives. The increasing commoditization of financial products means that in future investment alternatives will be extensive. Obviously, investors will have to choose those that offer the potential of significant returns for their personal time horizon and established risk profile. Liquidity issues will also be important. While real estate funds may show good returns, investors will also need funds that can be more liquid, just in case they must withdraw funds in the event of an unforeseen need for cash. Equally, the "onshore" nature of most prime real estate means that values may be threatened by an increasing move offshore by many sovereign individuals, while the fund may also be endangered by future predatory government activity.

Hedge funds and CTAs will become increasingly homogenous in the early decades of the new millennium. There will also be a host of new specialist funds with scopes ranging from the very narrow right through to the broadest imaginable. Already the sports and leisure boom throughout the world has led to a series of funds being established with narrow focuses, such as investing only in soccer clubs. Such funds have been created as unit trusts, and even hedge-fund structures. The classic unit trust will find itself struggling to survive if its fee structures are not reduced, or radically revised. In the Capital Market Revolution, entitlement fees for management will be radically downsized.

Performance is emphasized by all parties in the New Reality, with incentivized fees being the norm. The up-front 5 percent unit trust loading fee is excessive in the cyber age. Such fees will rapidly be eliminated as increasing numbers of new offshore cyber funds find their much lower overhead bases allow them to reduce significantly and ultimately eliminate such up-front loadings. Similarly, redemptions will be increasingly available online, so reducing the often substantial bid/offer spreads current in many unit trusts. With unit trust prices becoming more readily available online for the likes of index trackers, it is only a matter of time before the single daily redemption price gives way to perhaps twice-daily price "fixings." Eventually, it will not surprise us to see live prices on the Internet for dealing in index tracker funds. This can only help to reduce bid/offer entry/exit spreads as arbitrageurs will quickly close down price discrepancies using derivatives and cash baskets against the existing tracker funds. Indeed, the case of the Dow Jones-tracking Diamonds offered on NASDAQ (via AMEX) is an example of an index tracker already freely available on an exchange. The vagaries of fair-value calculation and the existing illiquidity of many bid/offer spreads in underlying stocks mean that index tracker fund bid/offers will probably not be as low as they are in futures or options markets (where one tick or 0.01 has become increasingly commonplace in liquid contracts). Nevertheless, it will reduce significantly from up to 500 basis points for OTC fund offerings at present to probably only 10 or 20 basis points in the relatively near future. Ultimately, smaller bid/offer spreads in the more liquid funds will be possible.

The new funds

"The small will flourish in this new environment because they have always been at the periphery and they have economies of scope and the ability to make quick decisions. They have speed. In the old economy speed was not so critical. Today it is everything."

John Naisbitt, *Global Paradox*

In the new millennium the reduced costs of entering the funds management markets will bring in a vast array of new marketplaces and hugely innovative means of managing risk and providing portfolio returns. The most exciting innovations will be offshore. This will be a largely unregulated (or at most very lightly regulated) market, unless regulators manage miraculously to lose their plodding heavy-handed approach (commonplace in domestic markets) and suddenly understand the benefits of soft regulation, bureaucratic speed (if that isn't a contradiction that strikes at the very heart of regulators' ethos!) and a new-found capacity to make fast decisions. In other words, the New Reality is an enormous threat to regulators. We will examine this in more detail later.

The most exciting innovations will be offshore.

Those investors who seek regulatory protection will be able to deal onshore, but it will cost them a significant premium. Admittedly, dealing offshore will bring some greater risks because of the relatively lax regulatory regime. Having said that, the offshore locale which manages to provide an even-handed and relatively simple-to-administer regulatory regime, giving some protection to investors without hampering investment managers, will be poised to reap huge rewards for their island or state. In the Capital Market Revolution, regulators are under threat of extinction unless they learn fast how to evolve away from narrow nationalistic borders.

> "Time zones, taxes and the regulatory regime are the only impediments to investment nowadays. Borders no longer exist."
>
> **Paul Davis, Fund Manager, Tech Invest**

Onshore funds, saddled with extra regulatory burdens, will still exist but their costs of doing business will be significantly higher. Such costs will have to be borne by investors who prefer the comfort of regulation.

In the Capital Market Revolution, funds to invest in all sorts of markets will be possible. Geographical specialization is already commonplace, although this will increase as even tiny regions are targeted by specialist niche managers. The old narrow nationalist borders will increasingly shrink from many investment horizons, in line with Paul Davies' "borders no longer exist" thesis. In the future, one will not merely invest in Italy, but rather in the Prato textile region, or even the development of Liguria. Similarly, there will be funds devoted to investing in the technology of racing cars. Indeed, Patrick Young is not alone amongst those who have produced draft prospectuses for funds to invest in classic cars in recent years. In the mid-1980s a leading classic-car dealer, Chris Drake, almost succeeded in listing a vehicle to invest in classic cars on the London Stock Market. Ironically, the venture would have shown staggering returns in the subsequent classic-car bubble of the latter years of the decade.

> Any feature of fund management, investment, or stock brokerage will increasingly be available from a series of one-stop shops on the Internet.

"NewVas" will result in funds devoted to everything from the very largest industry groups right through to micro-operations. The venture capital business will be hugely affected by this enterprise – as we will see later.

All these bells and whistles will be instantly available to an online trader through the World Wide Web. Switching funds will become sheer simplicity. Already many single functional operations are available. However, in the future, investors will be able to do all their personal financial applications and their investments online, with a capacity to move their mortgage and other debt financing back and forth as and when they need to add duration to their portfolio, or append some form of gearing. Any feature of fund management, investment, or stock brokerage will increasingly be available from a series of one-stop shops on the Internet.

Tied agencies are dead

In retail financial services, thanks to the Capital Market Revolution, integration is becoming serious in a way nobody would have conceived of a few years ago. Similar to our NewVas-broker model within derivatives and stock markets, the new-age financial services sales manager will become a much more sophisticated animal, advising a much broader array of customers. Increasing commoditization of all policies (including life insurance, assurance, and endowments) will be simpler to buy (and indeed resell in the after-market). The increasing commoditization of such products will have a very significant impact on commissions. Brokers will see their returns dwindling on each sale, as increased cross-border competition pushes broker returns down. Such dwindling returns will also prompt financial services retailers to adopt much leaner organizations with far fewer staff. There will be many more customers per salesperson (thanks to allowing the customers increased access to electronic decision-making tools via the Internet). This will also mean that the commissions payable for many insurance products will be dramatically reduced, as increased competition kills the old-style tied agents.

Equally, the old-style insurance and financial planning salesperson will be able to offer much more extensive services at little extra cost. Depending on the regulatory regime under which they operate, a financial services retailer will be able to add a stock, bond, commodity, futures, and options brokerage overnight, by simply signing up to a brokerage franchise plan such as that offered by Jean-Yves Sireau's Mr Market operation as discussed in Chapter 5.

Similarly, where before there were often significant fiscal advantages to being tied to one of the old localized leviathans of fund management, the new retail broker will find the need to be fast and flexible in line with the "NewVas" model. Brokers will want to pick and choose from a vast array of global financial services, many of which are provided by small boutique operations. This is one area where disintermediation of financial services may be seen to operate in reverse. However, the costs will be so slight for customer and vendor that the returns will hugely benefit both parties. Similarly, tiny boutique fund managers will now be able to market to the world through their own Web sites and a network of agents all signed up with a minimum of fuss on a *pro bono* basis. Regulators will initially attempt to lash out at such activity via the Internet, as they see their turf being virtually invaded, but ultimately they too must reform or die.

Bottlenecks in the system

CTA/hedge-fund operators with innovative new ideas and an impresive track record will become increasingly difficult to find (by 2005 at the latest). Indeed, by 2001 there may already be significant bottlenecks in the system. A new format for ascertaining good money managers will have to be discerned within this industry. At present, many fund allocators are themselves alarmingly little more than sheep in the allocation process. The demand for vast swathes of statistics to justify decisions has led to a large skewing in favor of traders who can trade entirely automated methods. While system traders will continue to grow within the New Reality, thanks to the continuing growth in computing power, the fact remains that the best money managers in history – such as Warren Buffett (Berkshire Hathaway), Julian Robertson (Tiger), and George Soros (Quantum)[4] *et al.* – are invariably discretionary managers who take decisions based upon a system that contains a vast array of variables and is implemented by human inputs rather than automated on computers. Commodity Pool Operators (CPOs) and other hedge-fund allocators need to rethink their own way of doing business with new and smaller funds if they are not to find a chronic under-capacity of managers with a severe oversupply of funds trying to find their way into the CTA/hedge fund programs.

Similarly, the money allocators will have to get away from what seems to be a substantial fear of investing with (discretionary) global macrofunds. In an era where communications are so far superior to anything yet seen in history, global macrofunds' management will be vital to the new money managers. Allocators need to stop eschewing such advisors, as they will doubtless succeed in finding different niches across the world from many of their counterparts. In addition, absolutely the best returns in history have been achieved by global macro managers. To eschew this whole area of investing, because allocators are concerned about their jobs, is frankly farcical. This area of the allocation business needs to be addressed and reformed rapidly. Those who do so fastest will find themselves in pole position to get the best choice of the new wave of fund managers in an era of unprecedented growth. This growth splurge will simply be explosive, starting by 2001 (if not sooner) and lasting for up to a decade. The explosive rise in alternative fund managers will precisely mirror the crumbling decline to be experienced by the existing conventional large-money managers whose stranglehold on investment close to the cusp of the new millennium had threatened a protracted period of dominance. Some will survive. Many brands will probably be snapped up by cheeky hedge funds seeking to add to their marketing muscle through using a household name. However, the leviathans of today's investment management are largely doomed to oblivion and national obscurity in the future.

> **This area of the allocation business needs to be addressed and reformed rapidly.**

Regulation – always close to the surface of the problem

Another problem that is already perfectly visible to observers and practitioners alike of the "new alternative" money managers is that of regulation. Several CTAs with perfectly plausible track records have already been forced to rethink their business (and indeed in several instances, forced out of business altogether) by the regulatory regime in which bureaucracy is seen as a way to save everybody from risk. The reality is that small onshore CTAs are being frustrated by vast quantities of pointless paperwork, a situation that was worsened for European CTAs by the EU imposing various investment directives during the late 1980s and early 1990s. Stories of European CTAs spending half their day's business dotting "i"s and crossing "t"s to satisfy faceless bureaucrats are commonplace. Such a situation endangers the good operation of a CTA. Unless a fund manager can be free to research and trade with as little input from regulators as possible, the CTA business will die.

Despite the foibles of the LTCM débâcle, regulating hedge funds is little more than a tragic specter of regulators seeing their remits dwindle and making a turf grab in reaction. Increasingly, the large allocators will bring in more requests for hedge funds to be more transparent about their levels of gearing, which will largely eliminate the concerns raised by LTCM. Such allocators have the leverage to achieve more prudent funds management, which regulators can only envy. Meanwhile, the

> Unless a fund manager can be free to research and trade with as little input from regulators as possible, the CTA business will die.

CTA and smaller hedge funds will increasingly find themselves being nurtured offshore. The concept of a CTA trading "school" operated from a suitably interesting offshore location such as Monaco must surely be a working proposition in the near future. It would give brokers a regular income stream from essentially captive business while the fund managers would have back-office staff on hand, alongside experienced money management consultants to provide advice and to coach traders where required. Such a situation would also provide a great opportunity for the institution sponsoring the initiative not only to have future upside through equity participation with the CTAs but also to gain significant brokerage rewards. Certainly, the influence of the big fundamental money managers will never regain the near-monopoly position of financial assets they attained in the late 1980s and early 1990s.

Bottlenecks will occur amongst the ranks of the new alternative managers. Nevertheless, the future upside for the alternative money managers is awesome. Their capacity for managing up to and beyond hundreds of millions of dollars each, using compact flexible management teams, is the way of the future. If stock markets are not sufficiently liquid for such funds to invest, then they will seek ways to replicate holdings through derivatives, or some other method-ology that affords an easier investment. Some funds will specialize in holding such illiquid investments. However, in the information age, it is more likely that many funds will hold smaller parcels of stock in companies on transparent exchanges. Stock-market liquidity will also be aided by the biggest change of the New Reality – the vast move away from corporatizing assets through massive-fund managers, with a significant quantity of funds flowing back to the control of private client traders.

The remarkable rise of the private client

Communism has long promised but invariably failed to deliver "power to the people". Now capitalism, and free-market capitalism in its essentially undistilled form, is giving individuals the chance to shape their financial destiny with better flows of information and access to markets than have ever been witnessed at any previous time in history. At its epicenter, the Capital Market Revolution gives private investors the opportunity to take control of their finances in a way that has never before been clearly afforded to them. The revolution provides private capital with all the tools it requires to take on large institutional funds and beat them.

> The revolution provides private capital with all the tools it requires to take on large institutional funds and beat them.

It won't be a walkover, but at least now the deck will become less stacked against the individual. Thanks to the New Reality", the private individual will become more pivotal than ever before.

There have been ebbs and flows of mass involvement in the stock market before, such as in the 1920s when the public largely lost out in the Great Crash. In the aftermath of the capital market revolution, investors will have to be talented enough to exploit their newly acquired advantages to make healthy profits. The opportunity is there – and it is stronger than it has ever been in history.

Throughout the post-war era, the increasing intervention by government in financial markets has seen the tax system skewed to favor massive, blundering investment corporations, while the public has largely been brainwashed into thinking that these self-same large funds are the best way to gain an edge in financial markets. But as we have already detailed, the results overall are generally somewhat woeful – especially since these are the results made by the so-called professional experts! The fact of the matter is that investors have grown increasingly suspicious of large fund managers, who seem to demand extortionate up-front fees for little reward and a considerable amount of risk.

In the information age the world of work is changing. Teleworking, freelancing, and other forms of working from home are becoming more popular. Self-employment will increasing become the norm amongst those who wish to be financially secure. It will have all the usual concomitant risks, but the wages to be earned from onshore wage slavedom will become less and less attractive as desperate governments squeeze the bourgeoisie "until the pips squeak". Equally, the number of early retirees will increase – some voluntary, others enforced by the incapacity of many corporations to see the benefits of employing experienced, mature citizens because they are not as cheap as less educated, less experienced youths (the increasing desperation of government to get youth unemployment down while letting the more mature citizens flounder plays a part here). The pool of capital acquired by these retirees through a working life – and often topped up by redundancy – will add significantly to the potential pool of investment funds to be invested. With time on their hands, such individuals are already increasingly honing their investment skills.

The new playing field for financial investment is much more level. It allows vast quantities of information to be disseminated to any trader anywhere in the world within seconds. Paper-based publications are already seeing their margins eroded through the rapid accessibility of electronic media. For instance, there are various derivatives publications available monthly on paper across the world. However, many cost several hundred dollars per annum. In contrast, the *Applied Derivatives Trading* project, begun by Tony

Webb and Patrick Young, can disseminate information monthly via the World Wide Web at http://www.adtrading.com for free. It is difficult to think of a better price to pay for information. What's more, the information is not merely free, it is global the instant the new issue is published on the first of the month. Readers in 128 countries worldwide receive *ADT* as soon as it is published. Paper publications can typically take days to reach even local addresses, and may take weeks to get to the other side of the world.

As with monthlies, so too with hard news. Admittedly, information flow is only as good as the reporting and in some countries getting information out will remain an imperfect art for years to come. For example, in Italy financial news traditionally percolates around a network in Rome for a while, then reaches the Milanese banks, and it may be a few hours before it finally breaks out of the cycle of going from bank to bank. Whilst such information seepage will probably continue, the Internet means the timings are increasingly being reduced before an announcement is made official.

> **Market access is now becoming ever simpler for all manner of products across the globe.**

Market access is now becoming ever simpler for all manner of products across the globe. The fact that local brokers can use a system like Mr Market to add a global end to their existing stockbrokerage business is an enormous boon to the private investor. Equally, the increasing pressure on derivatives brokers and clearing agents to entice more business – because electronic trading provides lower margins – will lead to wider access to all manner of commodity markets for any individual with the necessary cash. Now it will be possible to beat the giants in a David and Goliath struggle, played out on a largely level pitch.

The amazing rise of the online broker

> "The new investor class is neither uninformed nor naïve. Financial information is both cheap and accessible, whether the source be a newspaper, television or the Internet. Investors are also well served by an army of financial planners, stockbrokers, economists, and fund managers. Individual investors know what they are doing, and they cheerfully accept personal responsibility for their decisions."
>
> **Lawrence Kudlow, Chief Economist, American Skandia Life Assurance Inc.**

Born in the USA, online investing is a massive growth business. According to research by Credit Suisse First Boston Electronic Commerce analyst, Bill Burnham, the total online trading generated in 1996 was some 268 million US dollars. By 1998 this had grown to 1.67 billion dollars. By 2001 a figure of 2.3 billion dollars is being predicted. This figure is even more staggering when it is borne in mind that the online brokers charge significantly lower commissions than their old-fashioned "full-service" cousins. Something like 25 percent of retail trades were conducted online in 1998; by 2001 Burnham predicts this will grow to almost two-thirds of all retail brokerage commissions. Another study suggested some 700 billion dollars in assets will be held in some 14 million online brokerage accounts in the USA alone. If anything, we believe this is probably a low estimate, as many commentators still do not take the growth of Total Online Investment Management By Individual Solutions (TOMBIS) into account. TOMBIS will mean individuals taking total control of their assets. As the Internet's own brand of radical disintermediation helps individuals manage all their assets online, TOMBIS will mark an explosion of online asset management. The market may easily be worth as much as 2 billion US dollars by 2002. Thereafter, compounded growth of 20+ percent in online trading is perfectly feasible.

Pitfalls of avarice

"All of us think of ourselves as rational beings even in times of crisis, applying the laws of probability in cool and calculated fashion to the choices that confront us. We like to believe we are above-average in skills, intelligence, farsightedness, experience, refinement, and leadership. Who admits to being an incompetent driver, a feckless debater, a stupid investor, or a person with an inferior taste in clothes?"

Peter Bernstein, *Against the Gods*

Private investors who survive the grueling pace of professional investment will need to be trained like samurai in the art of investment.

In *Seeing Tomorrow – Rewriting the Rules of Risk*, Ron Dembo and Andrew Freeman quote the behavioral economist Meir Statman, bluntly addressing the risk facing the private investor when he enters the ring after some amateur bouts to contest a few rounds with the professionals:

Most investors simply cannot see that they are the suckers in the game. The real suckers are the ones who think they can divine inside information from the *Wall Street Journal*. For example, they might read an article about ageing baby boomers who need bifocals and think they can make a buck by buying shares in an eyewear company. But they are usually just observing something that lots of other people already know.[5]

Private investors who survive the grueling pace of trading with the professionals will need to be trained intensively in the art of investment. They will of course be helped by an increasing range of training courses and seminars put on by the successful pros. Alas, there will also be a lot of substandard material, peddled by those who are affectionately referred to as "snake oil" vendors by many trading professionals. Certainly, a worrying aspect to the Internet stock boom of the late 1990s was that so many private client traders looked alarmingly as if they were being driven more by the "greater fool" theory than anything else.[6]

Many private clients will need a considerable amount of application if they want to be in a position to trade with the experts. However, given how many months it takes to be able to cook like a cordon bleu chef, the road to being a competent trader is probably somewhat easier. What's more, only the truly exceptional cook can become a genuine cordon bleu chef. Armed with a judicious dose of discipline and reasonable application, just about any reasonably capitalized individual has the opportunity to make it as a professional trader.

The wonders of Internet trading

The Internet has of course been the means by which anybody can now trade the London, or New York, or Tokyo, or Sydney markets, regardless of whether they are at home in Bathurst in New South Wales, Killarney in the Irish Republic, or the Moroccan city of Tangiers. Electronic markets are the only way to go for order-entry across the globe.

Traders will have a variety of means of electronic entry to the markets. The simplest is the Internet access. As we have seen, firms such as E-Trade, Schwab Online, and so forth have enjoyed exponential growth in their services since they began Internet trading in the late 1990s. Yet their prospects are barely past the elementary development stages. Nevertheless their impact has already been awesome. Private clients are suddenly increasing their proportion of the market share in securities-trading for the first time in the post-war period. Internet trading offers a number of significant advantages compared to the old-fashioned concept of speaking to a broker. For a start, the broker is never engaged. True, momentary bottlenecks can occur in the Internet but these only delay dealing by a few seconds. Private clients will never again suffer the problem of being unable to get in contact with their brokers as was the case worldwide for traders during the stock market crash of 1987.

The fact is that the Internet gives all traders essentially equal access to prices and trades throughout the financial markets at any time of the day and night, regardless of borders, time zones and geography. Indeed, the online brokers themselves have already noted interesting phenomena during acute periods of market volatility, such as in late 1997 and 1998 when global equities wobbled. At that time those lucky holders of online trading accounts found themselves with such high-quality access to the exchanges that some took to acting as a form of intermediary for their friends saddled with old-style speak-to-a-broker accounts. The "full service" clients ironically found themselves unable to deal,

Both brokers and traders will benefit froam such electronic trading.

as their snowed-under sales brokers could not answer phone calls fast enough to process the incoming orders. This "throttling" bottleneck will be eradicated by increasing numbers of traders going online.

For those traders who wish to step up a gear, or who are more interested in trading intraday in volatile commodities and futures markets, etc., there are already a number of excellent opportunities afforded by terminals that can be placed at home, or in an office (or even on a laptop for those who mix office ISDN use with some Internet access). Such screens are available at a variety of price levels. For instance, the trader may use an ISDN line which links them into the rear of the system at their brokers. Costs will be cheap, since the orders from those in the brokerage may come in faster and ahead of this "rear" client. To be at the very front end where orders go straight to the exchange will require different routing and a premium expense. For those traders who want the ultimate speed of access then the premium route will be the way to go. Nevertheless, even those on the lowest electronic access levels can still have marginally better execution than they were used to with existing offline brokers.

Both brokers and traders will benefit from such electronic trading. For the brokers, risks can be managed much more easily (i.e. position limits can be enforced by simply refusing orders where the traders try to overstep their limits, or deal when they have insufficient funds in their account, or sell stock that they do not have held in escrow/cleared with that broker, etc.). For the trader, account statements will be available online and account balances can be updated within minutes of dealing. Such automation of position holdings will greatly help both the risk-management and margin functions of a broker, as well as allowing traders to see their positions in real time.

There are only online discounted brokers

Some brokers may be more discounted than others, but those who remain haughtily aloof from the discounted broker revolution will soon find themselves out of business. The entire commoditization process of securities dealing means that the very concept of old-style stockbrokers charging vast premiums for their services will be eroded very rapidly. The only brokers able to survive will be those who incorporate the "NewVas" principles into their business practices. Whilst clients will pay a little more for some additional input, companies will no longer be able to expect a vast premium for their research. Indeed, thanks to mass publishing entities such as the Internet, research that was formerly guarded judiciously for the largest institutional customers will increasingly become widely available to private clients. Once again, the New Reality playing field in the new millennium will be a great deal more flat than the old corporatized structure from the post-war era.

A new blueprint for a new local

"Locals can and are beginning to use electronic systems effectively."
Roz Wilton, MD Transaction Products, Reuters PLC

"Open outcry works as well as it does because of the locals. They are the ones that supply the bids as the market looks for a bottom. They are the ones that scalp the market, providing the liquidity, keeping the spreads in line.

Why are locals willing to do that? Why do they take those risks? They do it because they make money at it. The reason they make money is that they have an advantage by virtue of the fact that they stand in the pit. They see and hear and feel things traders away from the floor can't sense. The successful locals can turn this extra information into enough of an advantage to make a living."

Wendell Kapustiak, Director of Global Futures Operations, Merrill Lynch

Roz Wilton's statement, dating back to mid-1997, highlights an aspect to financial markets that has been of some concern to individuals and institutions alike. Independent traders on the floor of an exchange – "locals" as they are referred to in trading parlance – are as old as the trading floors themselves. The local has traditionally provided liquidity in exchange for being able to trade on the floor of the exchange. This geographical proximity to the market helped locals profit. It was also a great advantage to be able to watch order flow entering the pit and then trade in the direction of the orders. This sort of "front running" to the market gave an advantage to the faster institutions and penalized the slow – which, after all, is the kind of Darwinian competition that sport and trading are all about. Locals were fortunate in that pit orders could not be precisely prioritized by the time they arrived in the marketplace. Therefore, locals could simply lift the offers to buy the market as they wanted when they needed to be aggressive and move the market (or vice versa when they wished to sell). This lovely advantage has been removed by electronic systems where the exchanges are imposing a first-in, first-out order-execution system. For locals trading in an electronic age, the cream has gone.

> **For locals trading in an electronic age, the cream has gone.**

The evolving local realpolitik

The annual FIA expo in Chicago is an opportunity to showcase the derivatives industries' new technological applications. However, during these November gatherings in the Windy City in the 1990s, the reactionary nature of some Chicago locals became increasingly polarized.

Those who say that locals are written off are either abjectly misinformed, or institutional employees who feel acutely jealous of the fortunes accrued by the best of the independent pit traders. The fact is that locals now have a tremendous opportunity to profit from the New Reality. However, they will have to substantially modify their dealing styles and their thought processes. Locals who cannot manage such fundamental re-engineering will find themselves out of business. However, there will be others who will readily fill this space. The e-locals will flourish in the new environment, especially as they will be able to diversify risk and explore new opportunities in a vast array of different markets, all of which can now be traded electronically from the comfort of wherever they wish to be.

The trading arcade concept – undertaken by major local clearer Kyte Futures in London and organizations like LQuay far from the pre-revolution mainstream in Sydney – will be a core meeting place for those locals who enjoy the social side of trading. One downside to trading alone at home is that it can be a remarkably solitary experience. It suits some, but will not suit many existing locals. New trading arcades will spring up wherever a community of locals wishes to support them. In the UK, many will open at the junctions of the M25 motorway around London, for instance to the east, which is close to Essex and where many established LIFFE locals live. Equally, arcades will prove popular in tax havens where locals can keep their profits away from governments which seek to impose swingeing taxes and which have yet to understand what the New Reality means for them.

Interestingly, when MATIF first went electronic, the exchange actually found itself initially adding capacity from locals soon after the move to screen-based trading. Local volume moved from 15 to

20 percent of exchange volume totals (comparing the initial electronic trading period to the latter months of open outcry). Some 20 new locals joined the exchange to trade exclusively electronically soon after the market closed the floor.

The e-local primer

> "Current electronic systems filter out the intelligence that is a local's stock-in-trade. The information available to an electronic trader today is so distilled, so simplified, so sparse as to take the locals' advantage away. With current terminals, current bandwidth, current software technology, however, a willing market could reproduce much of the essence of open outcry trading within an electronic system."
>
> **Wendell Kapustiak, Director of Global Futures Operations, Merrill Lynch**

The original electronic LIFFE after-hours APT system included many of the facets recomended by Kapustiak. Alas, since then exchange electronic systems have been rather drab affairs, showing various bids, offers, and little more. Such a lack of transparency is a bad sign for derivatives markets. The greater the transparency, the easier it is for market makers to feel enticed into trading. The centerpiece of the digital age has been the broader dissemination of information. Electronic exchanges must address the information equation by

The greater the transparency, the easier it is for market makers to feel enticed into trading.

providing at least as much data as was previously available to the local – counterparty bid/offers and details of execution, with the computer tallying the information easily on screen to aid calculation. Ironically, the latter information can be much more precise on electronic exchanges.

The most successful electronic systems will be those that provide a "feel" for the market. For instance, an indicator of how many traders tried to hit their bid or lift their offer will give an e-local a very handy indicator of how the market is facilitating trade, as well as demonstrating just how interested different counterparties actually are in trading. On a screen that shows the number of traders occupying a pit, it can be difficult to discern how (if at all) interested such traders actually are in facilitating transactions. In the electronic age, this is especially true as traders may be logged into screens with little more than a "watching brief". In contrast, the local can always discern the actively interested traders in a pit, as those merely watching the world trade by will tend to loiter on the edges or keep signaling order flow back to the booth without actually processing orders.

The ultimate screens

"The only choices are not open-outcry on one hand, and today's austere electronic systems on the other. The focus should be on why the current pit-traded markets work as well as they do, and try to retain those essential features on the screen."

Wendell Kapustiak, Director of Global Futures Operations, Merrill Lynch

The trading systems of the future will ultimately exist in virtual reality. The LIFFE exchange demonstrated a virtual trading floor at the Chicago expo in the mid-1990s. The opportunity to meld human dynamism with the sheer processing power of future computers should create an ideal market environment. However, in the interim, computer systems of the next decade need to focus on making as much information as possible flow back to traders. Some analysts see this as a means by which electronic locals will gain an added advantage. This is simply reincorporating the foibles of the old system in to the New Reality. Rather, in the new era of a completely alternative and almost entirely flat playing field, the market must disseminate as much information as possible to all participants. The information age gives all participants a more level playing field. To give any particular group an in-built advantage just to satisfy past tribal hierarchies is utterly asinine – whether the group be equity block traders, or futures locals. Although on stock markets it may take some time for the mantra of liquidity to be fully equated with transparency, at least in the New Reality if existing market mechanisms are unwilling to tackle their failings, new mechanisms will rapidly spring up to deal with such flaws – removing the existing business with it and potentially dealing a fatal blow to the exchange.

Until now, electronic trading systems have largely relied on alphanumeric visual signals to indicate what is happening in a market. By themselves, these are very limited. Future systems will incorporate sound and better use of colors to provide information. When a market bid is being hit simultaneously by a large number of participants, then what better indicator could there be than a noise that can modulate according to the quantity of people trying to trade? Similarly, market-depth and order-flow indicators could show through bar charts or some other histogram form the quantity of orders entering electronic markets. These could move up and down through different colored regions, from blue for relatively few orders through to red for extreme numbers of orders entering the market at any one moment. Such systems have already been introduced to analyze existing foreign-exchange and derivatives markets by various in-house software development teams. We expect systems that require more than simply the capacity to read figures will increasingly become the norm during the first decade of the new millennium.

Even with such added bells and whistles, the e-local will have to work harder in the New Reality. The old fashioned "jobbers" who simply traded frequently across the bid and offer for tiny profits will find themselves severely restricted by the new law of first-in, first-out order filling. Jobbing is to all intents and purposes dead. Indpendent traders will need to find a niche in which they can outperform the institutions. For many traders this will still be an intraday trading process. However, instead of trading dozens of times a day, dealers will now trade only once or twice per day. At the most, traders are unlikely to trade regularly more than five or six times per day. Similarly, traders who have been used to trading large clip sizes across bid and offer will find that, to get their positions on and exit positions safely perhaps a few hours later, their position sizes may also have to be reduced.

Locals making the transition from open outcry to electronic trading need to analyze their trading skills carefully before making the move. Firstly, an exercise in income attribution is vital. One of the reasons the leading hedge funds are so brilliant over long periods of time is because they know precisely where they successfully profit. In pit trading – and in many other facets of trading – dealers spend too little time actually analyzing

> **Locals making the transition from open outcry to electronic trading need to analyze their trading skills carefully before making the move.**

where they make their money. Now, locals must look at their profits and see what they made and where. Because, remember, the cream has gone. There will be many locals who will disappear from the trading business because they bull-headedly believed trading could continue as it always has done. The e-local in the aftermath of the Capital Market Revolution will be a much more market-knowledgeable person. Greater analysis will be required to place trades profitably. Many floor traders will be reluctant to accept the need to improve skills. However, traders will invariably find that the new markets will require, if not major revisions, certainly minor reworking to their trading skills. That is not to say that all traders must become systemized and use some computer code to decide their trades for them. But there will need to be a great deal more input into their trading decisions. Nevertheless, the process of discretionary trading will remain a vital aspect of trading. Indeed, as more and more traders follow systemized computers for all their trading decisions, more opportunities will arise to make the discretionary trader a great deal of money. In the New Reality, change, flexibility, and a desire to rethink the basic trading approaches will be vital.

Liquidity impacts of the new locals

As Max Whitby gazed out of his George Street office window towards the Sydney Futures Exchange (SFE) just across the road, he realized that after 1999 things would never be the same again for his firm, his core clients, and indeed the Australian markets. Whitby is the Managing Director of LQuay, Australia's largest local clearing firm. Some 300 SFE locals utilized his clearing services during the last days of open outcry in Australia. Whitby, himself a long-standing pit trader, was sorry to see the process go, but he was also relishing the chance to work along the new frontier. When the SFE's CEO, Les Hosking, had announced the decision to go electronic in 1997, it had shocked many of the members. Cloak-and-dagger stories circulated about management reports being withheld from members. On the floor a host of badges were distributed bearing Hosking's image along with a series of increasingly derogatory slogans. Nevertheless, the SFE stood firm and it looked as if Les Hosking would be the first to steer his exchange from open outcry to electronic trading. As we have already discussed, the Paris MATIF pipped him at the post in early 1998.

Having seen the sands shifting on his regular visits to Europe and the US, Whitby prepared to deal with the Capital Market Revolution. His IT team created a complete new front-end interface that could be operated over an ISDN line or routed through the Internet to the LQuay offices and on to the exchange itself. Ironically, delays in implementing the SFE's new systems meant that the LQuay dealing software was operative before the open outcry era in Sydney ended. Nevertheless, Whitby was already vexed by how the whole dynamics of the trading and broking/clearing business could be changed by the move to electronic trading. He had good reason to be worried – the move to electronic trading can bring with it significantly different market and liquidity dynamics.

Firstly, the old pit trading, as we discussed, allowed locals to trade large clips regularly back and forth. On electronic systems, first-in, first-out execution rules mean that customers get a better deal, but the end users may find liquidity drained as locals find it harder to do the jobbing that formed the basis of their trading in the open outcry days. The liquidity hurdle is not the only problem. For local traders have long been used to paying tiny incremental charges per lot transacted for their clearing fees. Clearing agents could justify this because the locals regularly turned over large quantities of contracts (perhaps hundreds, even thousands for the biggest locals on the largest exchanges every day).[7] However, with first-in, first-out order priority, the locals have lost their cream and also the need to deal in the markets so frequently.

However, if the locals' turnover dwindles, then the whole pricing equation for clearing services needs to be re-addressed. Yesterday's 500-lot-a-day, 50-cent-to-clear-a-contract local may become tomorrow's 50-lot-a-day, 2-dollars-to-clear e-local. E-locals will not like to see their incremental costs rising. If clearing agents are to survive, they must adjust costs. With electronic markets creating added commoditization of every process, there have already been several small clearing agents in London who closed in the late 1990s, even before the full LIFFE Connect electronic system was introduced. So, clearing agents need to keep their revenues up and will probably have to raise their per unit prices when markets increasingly go electronic. Otherwise they face the prospect of lower trading volumes and with it lower revenues. Moreover, the lower trading volumes from locals may impact on liquidity as we mentioned above, so also leading to lower trading volumes from end users unable to execute business on exchanges, which in turn reduce the revenue to brokers and clearing agents.

> **If clearing agents are to survive, they must adjust costs.**

Furthermore, there may be many locals who have habitually tended to over-trade their agreed position limits but this could not be monitored by the clearing agents during the open outcry era. While electronic trading terminals can easily prevent such over-trading, the resultant losses of revenue may prove problematic for clearing agents. Equally, the Capital Market Revolution could be threatened by poor (i.e. overly risk-averse) compliance within large clearing agents or from regulatory remit where traders are forced to meet increasingly stringent demands for capital from regulators. Such demands may not just strangle the liquidity on exchanges but also threaten the livelihoods of traders who are still subject to such extreme fads of regulation. Of course, thanks to the wonderful information flow in the information age, the traders left onshore may soon find themselves severely outnumbered by their offshore brethren, who avoid not just increasingly punitive taxation but also the clutches of regulators. In the case of Max Whitby's Sydney LQuay organization, Internet/ISDN front-end software has been introduced in order to draw in a broader client base – of private clients and other interested parties from Australia and throughout Asia.

Exchanges will probably still make some concessions in order to promote specific contracts to locals and market-makers in institutions, for instance using fee holidays or rebates that support particular new contracts or help support flagging market. Nevertheless, in the New Reality the pressure will be on to maintain margins in clearing agents as they see their business potentially dwindling away. Meanwhile, the stock markets will increasingly find that they can add to liquidity by offering incentive discount programs for clearing and execution fees to those dealers who are able to add liquidity. Given the generally woefully inadequate state of liquidity in the equity market compared to futures markets, the introduction of more e-locals can only be a good thing.

The data revolution

Just as the new multimedia age assists the smallest independent traders, as the new playing field is much more level than its predecessor, so too the whole ethos of the information age may have significant effects on the finances of existing exchanges. In the late

1990s the CBOT typically received about 50 million US dollars in revenue for the sale of its quotes to dealers throughout the world. Exchanges have habitually charged a fee via the data vendors such as Reuters or Bloomberg for any market to which a trader has sought access. Indeed, when computer archival was more expensive during the 1980s and early 1990s, historical data was traditionally a rich resource that could be resold by vendors for significant premiums. Alas, the increasing digitization of common (and readily transferable) formats of data storage are already radically changing the way data is sold. End-of-day data purchased from some exchanges cost several dollars a month in the late 1990s yet already some other vendors had begun giving the same information away for free. This is increasingly going to happen with real-time data. In an environment where a niche exchange can spring up via the Internet or other electronic media within a matter of months, there will be increasing numbers of contracts competing for the trader's attention. True, some core dealers will invariably focus on particular markets and will be willing to pay the appropriate data fees. However, with markets increasingly needing to keep the liquidity providers happy, there will be many independent traders and e-locals who will tend to look at contracts in which they are given free access to the real-time feeds.

The Capital Market Revolution blows holes in existing exchange cash flows.

The Capital Market Revolution blows holes in existing exchange cash flows. Nowhere is this more graphically illustrated than in data vending fees. With the cost of disseminating prices falling all the time, exchanges were already offering limited live quotes via their Web sites in the late 1990s during the early stages of the Capital Market Revolution. Such free vending of quotations will continue to grow exponentially and will wreak havoc with the existing structures of established exchanges. This is because many markets, and especially those in Chicago, have grown used to selling their data in order to realize a profit. In the case of some exchanges, fees on contracts to members and users have been kept artificially low for the sake of placating the membership. Data fees may survive into the early years of the millennium, but by 2010 we expect the sale of live data to be largely extinct. There will be small charges for certain precious pieces of archived data, but this too will be a fraction of the cost of such services in the late 1980s and early 1990s. After all, online front-end trading systems such as PATS are not paying quote vendor fees for the data their clients use to trade with. So the question arises, why would a quote vendor continue to charge merely to look at such data when those using it for trading are getting it free?

There may be some new sources of revenue available to exchanges, such as increased returns from those outside issuers of OTC or on exchange products linked to particular indices (index tracker funds, etc.) where a fee will be paid for the use of the exchange's index. However, even these are unlikely to make up for the losses to be suffered from exchanges who find that in a truly competitive market, data cannot be sold at the sort of monopolistic prices that became a habit for some large markets during the 1980s.

The analyst John Naisbitt refers to information as "the crude oil that will fuel the economic engines of the twenty-first century."[8] Ironically, while information will also fuel the capital market revolution, this crude oil of multimedia is destined to become ever cheaper, if not almost entirely free. Those who cannot adjust to the New Reality will find this blows a catastrophic hole in their revenue projections.

Notes

1 Jess Lederman and Robert A. Klein (eds), *Hedge Funds*. This original hedge fund methodology was hugely successful for Alfred Jones. Indeed, Carol J. Loomis even wrote a feature for *Fortune Magazine* headlined "The Jones Nobody Keeps Up With".

2 Jess Lederman and Robert A. Klein (eds), *Hedge Funds*.

3 *Applied Derivatives Trading*, November 1998 Editorial, http:// www. adtrading. com, and also *L'Expansion*, 1 October 1998.

4 Soros's role at Quantum is a matter of some debate: while Soros himself has a prodigious capacity for managing money, his key attribute actually lies in

picking the right people (such as Henry Druckenmiller) to manage the Quantum coffers at appropriate stages of the investment cycle.

5 Ron Dembo and Andrew Freeman, *Seeing Tomorrow*.

6 The "greater fool" theory states that any investment is a good one provided you can always find a "greater fool" to buy it from you at a profit. Ultimately, when one runs out of fools to pay higher multiples, the market must collapse.

7 On an exchange marketing trip in Tokyo, a legendary CBOT local promised Japanese bankers he would make prices in 500 lots of US Treasury Bond futures if that would encourage them to deal on the exchange.

8 John Naisbitt, *Global Paradox*.

CHAPTER 7

The new meritocracy

How the Capital Market Revolution impacts upon the world at large

"But the most important effect of trading is that it keeps me linked to reality and truth. The beauty of the markets, and for me their quintessential characteristic, is that they are the final determinant of veracity. As Elmer Falker taught me, 'the markets tell the truth.' Washington policymakers, Tokyo or Berlin ministers, officials of governments the world over can try to tell the world whatever they want, but the markets tell the world the truth. It's that simple; no one can fool the market. Universally, government officials insist that their personal value judgement about the level of interest rates or the rate of their currency is the correct interpretation of the facts, but their opinion doesn't count a tinker's damn unless or until it is endorsed by the market."

Leo Melamed, *Escape to the Futures*

Never since Napoleon Bonaparte memorably established "opportunity for all" within his army and the French Empire, has there been more opportunity for any person, regardless of gender, race, or background, to profit. One of the primary areas where the information age will open up enormous opportunities and permit vast profits will be the world's financial markets. Just as the likes of Georges Danton profited from his speculation in the era of the French Revolution, for those with the capital, the initiative, and the drive to exploit the Capital Market Revolution, the potential rewards will be enormous. They will also be rewards that can be largely garnered at a rate of taxation that suits the achiever rather than placing the talented at the whim of rapacious governments. The Napoleonic slogan of "la carrière ouverte aux talents" will be a clarion call of those manning the barricades in the Capital Markets Revolution. Online, the opportunities for new model traders will abound, regardless of economic background.

The erosion of sovereignty

"Countries don't decide the value of their currency anymore. Individuals do. Sovereign states decided the value of their money and often printed as much as they liked. Now the approximately 22 000 currency traders with their computer screens make individual judgements about the relative value of a country's currency, and buy or sell millions of dollars with their clients' money and their money. These decisions are made largely on the basis of judgements about the economic viability of each country involved. And because they are backed up by very large bets and are not just casual options, they constitute a very good index of economic health. That is, the constantly shifting collective judgements of 22 000 individuals, with a large stake in the outcome, about the value of a country's currency against other currencies can probably be trusted more than most other judgements."

John Naisbitt, *Global Paradox*

If anything, Naisbitt may be understating the number of foreign exchange traders in the world. Nonetheless, he is absolutely correct in viewing how the power of individual traders now dictates what governments must decide. Of course this viewpoint does not support the politics of large government which is at the heart of most national and supranational leaderships on the cusp of the new millennium. Equally, it is a message often fed to the masses by the media without any real understanding of the situation.

The multimedia explosion, in conjunction with the Capital Market Revolution, is reshaping vast tracts of how the world works and interacts. The old politics of statist intervention, of government knowing best, and – above all – citizens being captives of their local regime by accident of birth, are all increasingly outmoded notions. English Internet guru and author of *Understanding Hypermedia 2000* Bob Cotton, puts it bluntly: "The free market just got freer."

> **Financial markets are not within the cyber economy, rather they are at its very core.**

The tyranny of distance, which made so many small businessmen peripheral to their counterparts in the next country, is largely over – provided you are within the cyber economy. Financial markets are not within the cyber economy, rather they are at its very core.

How to squander your advantage overnight

> "With a large and growing share of financial transaction occurring in cyberspace in the new millennium, individuals will have a choice of jurisdictions in which to lodge them. This will create intense competition to price government's services (the taxes it charges) on a nonmonopolistic basis. This is revolutionary."
>
> **James Dale Davidson and William Rees-Mogg,** *The Sovereign Individual*

The tiny island of Labuan, just off the coast of Borneo, may be the first victim of the politicians who have fallen foul of the Capital Market Revolution. Governed by Malaysia, the island is actually slightly closer to the oil-rich sultanate of Brunei. As a base for an oil refinery and a free port where Philippine and other South-East Asian merchant ships traditionally deal in all manner of cargoes, Labuan was a sleepy place, a tropical island with little history of note, aside from some frenzied activity in World War II. In 1996, when Patrick Young visited, the island was undergoing something of a rejuvenation.

In the 1990s Labuan was being rebuilt as an offshore financial services centre by the Malaysian government. With the aim of competing against Hong Kong and Singapore, Labuan offered corporations tax-free advantages similar to those of other tiny islands, such as the Isle of Man or the Channel Islands off the British mainland, Gibraltar off the coast of Spain, or the multiplicity of Caribbean islands that flourish near the east coast of the USA. The concept was a good one. While air links were poor (the only direct international flights came via Kuala Lumpur), a new airport was under construction and a financial park would be built. By 1996 the offices of the financial park were already filling up with various banks from not just Asia but Europe and further afield. New hotels had been built to cope with the financial visitors, while a small island was being turned into a mini-resort just outside Labuan harbour. The financial park had a pair of apartment blocks that were authorized for sale to foreigners on diagonally opposite corners, with offices filling the space between. The Malaysian government's plans for a "multimedia super corridor" included state-of-the-art digital links to the rest of the world and the Internet. Labuan was wired, it had state-of-the-art office blocks, and – except for a few staff complaining about the cost of local private school fees – there was little or nothing to quibble about in this purpose-built tax haven for the twenty-first century.

Ironically, having invited the leading powers of global capitalism to congregate and indeed base their South-East Asian financial operations from this tiny island haven, the Malaysians out-maneuvered themselves. When the Asian financial crisis hit in 1997, there were governments such as Thailand who took the financial markets' judgement on the chin and went on to redevelop their economies with a view to emerging from recession, stronger, better, and wealthier than their previous growth had achieved. In contrast, Malaysia's Dr Mahathir took the rather quirky route of denouncing the very capitalists who had helped Malaysia to unprecedented growth in the previous two decades. It was a death blow to the Labuan experiment. When the Malaysian government went further and actually took its currency out of the free-floating world system, it signed a death warrant on its credibility in the business of offshore finance. It was an ironic twist of fate: in the 1980s and early 1990s it had been well known in foreign-exchange circles that South-East Asian central banks such as Thailand, Malaysia, and others had been regular speculators in the world's foreign exchange markets. Suddenly, when the game went against them, Malaysia's government knocked the board over and ran out of the room in disgust. The Labuan concept was essentially stillborn just as it looked perfectly placed to be a niche offshore haven.

The Malaysian example will probably be repeated all too frequently by some governments who – while paying lip service to the multimedia explosion by laying cables – fail to understand the dynamics underpinning the entire Capital Market Revolution process. Even a sudden conversion in the Malaysian government back to the free market world would not necessarily rejuvenate the Labuan project. Financial markets, and especially offshore investors, demand fiscal and political stability. The schizophrenic nature of the latter days of the Mahathir regime did insurmountable damage to the Labuan project. Governments the world over need to realize that in the global electronic era they must demonstrate objective, strong, and sensible leadership. Cheap populism will serve only to hand a greater advantage to the smaller, more nimble governments of the world.

> **Governments the world over need to realize that in the global electronic era they must demonstrate objective, strong, and sensible leadership.**

If a government oversteps the mark of growth, or runs too high a deficit, then it cannot expect (regardless of how impressive its growth figures) to remain impervious to the forces of financial gravity. When financial speculators gather to push a currency over and there are fundamentals to underpin the market, then other speculators will sense the value in that market and stem the flow of selling. This is the simplest factor of market behavior, yet one that governments and some journalists refuse to understand for fear of exposing just how poorly managed an economy has been. With the Capital Market Revolution fostering power to the people on the new playing field, more individuals will be able to become involved in the dynamics of currency depreciation in the future, either shoring up a market or pushing that currency down. In either case, the law of the jungle will rule. Where there is some appropriate value, the market will find it. There may be momentary over- or under-valuations but these will be eased out – just as when parking a car we can be too close to the car in front before we gradually readjust our position in the space.

To avoid oblivion, governments will have to understand the dynamics of the global economy.

Farewell nation state

> "The development of networked information technology threatens to undermine the foundation, power and authority of the nation state. The result will be a continuing fragmentation of the state as economic power is transferred to the cyberstate. Britain will be reduced to little more than a large property management company, while the experts in information technology will form an international free-floating pool of talent generating unprecedented wealth."
>
> **Dr Stephen Mooney, London School of Economics, at the "Governance of Cyberspace" conference, 17 April 1997**

What Dr Mooney sees affecting Britain will affect every existing nation state in the world. For the dynamics of the Capital Market Revolution mean that the existing nation state can no longer hold together. In the new millennium, the growth of countries will be explosive. At the moment, almost one in four of the world's population lives in China. Soon they will live in a range of different smaller independent states. The same will be true of the Indian nation and even Europe. Information freedom favors the small and this will be as true of countries as it will be of corporations. Different dynamics may power break-ups on the surface, but the main force will be the information revolution. With capital markets able to adjust ever faster in an electronic age, new countries will find it easy to come to the market and fund their programs. Of course, this will be funding of programs within reason – capital markets will be the arbiters of good economics. Governments who are unwilling to abide by these rules will find themselves railing against capitalism and ultimately railing against their people who have grown tired of paying the capital price for prime ministerial arrogance and ineptitude.

> "We are moving toward a world where the capital markets constrain what governments can do – not the other way round. In this environment, government policy is influenced in real time by whether or not it makes economic sense. Bad policies will carry real penalties, and good policies will be quickly rewarded."
>
> **Lowell Bryan and Diana Farrell, *Market Unbound***

Of course governments will be reluctant to accept such a situation. Indeed politicians appear largely oblivious to change. They are unable to comprehend either the triumph of individuality or the ongoing march of globalization. Those who cannot accept change will wither and face an abyss. Meanwhile, those who demonstrate the capacity to be flexible and innovate while maintaining government spending at a fraction of their current levels will prosper. Alas, those politicians will be relatively few.

Those who cannot accept change will wither and face an abyss.

Like him or loathe him (and you cannot ignore him), Umberto Bossi, the leader of the Italian Northern League may never get to lead an independent state. But it is highly likely his State of the River Po, Padania, will happen if Italy cannot manage to get its big government's all-encompassing taxation and over-regulation under control. Ironically, the big threat for Bossi in reaching his dream of a separate Northern Italian state may be if the north of Italy fails to achieve a cohesive model and the old city states such as Genoa and

Venice go their own way, further fragmenting the Italian nation. In the UK, Scottish independence can only be aided by the devolution that the UK's Labour government hoped might help their power base there. Even in a relatively underpopulated state such as Australia, we expect the Capital Market Revolution will bring about substantial internal pressures within the barely century-old federation.

> "My gripe with the nation state is that it is just the wrong size – it does not mesh with the digital form of the future. Most nations are too big to be local, and all nations are too small to be global"
>
> **Nicholas Negroponte, Director MIT Media Laboratory**

Western Australia already has a small secessionist movement. As the central government in the Eastern states tries to use the mineral resources of the west to prop up its 1960s tax-and-spend policies, the West's population will finally cry "enough." It may not be before 2030, but ultimately the Australian federation looks shaky unless the Canberra politicians concentrate on running the country rather than profligate spending policies. In fact Australia has one of the few politicians in the entire world who might actually manage to succeed in the New Reality. Jeff Kennett, the state Prime Minister of Victoria, has rejuvenated Melbourne and its surrounds. Working from a very low base in the late 1980s, it is now a world-class venue for business relocation, with a thriving local economy, all thanks to merciless deregulation, strong business incentivization, and a considerable orientation towards the multimedia age. Governments worldwide could take a valuable lesson from Kennett's pro-growth, pro-market policies. If the whole of Australia or a really large trading nation could benefit from his skills, that nation would be in pole position to prosper from the Capital Market Revolution.

This leads to the tricky question of just which jurisdictions will have a promising future in the new millennium. Australia is definitely one of them (particularly so if Jeff Kennett gains national control). The country is remote geographically but, with the correct government in place, it could take on the world – using deregulation and a more global commercial approach. At present, there are still too many niggling impediments to commerce to make the country really worth the hassle of relocation. In the event of a separation of the nation, then provided the Kennett legacy continues, we predict Victoria will become a hiving multimedia hub for much of Asia in the twenty-first century. If regulation can be kept to offshore levels, then the small hedge funds and other financiers will increasingly base at least some of their trading operations in lifestyle-oriented areas such as Perth (provided it has strong government) and other parts of Southern Western Australia, such as Albany (as well as Victoria).

> **As financial markets become increasingly electronic, we expect to see more and more assets clustering offshore.**

As financial markets become increasingly electronic, we expect to see more and more assets clustering offshore. Especially in the early years of the new millennium, as the nation states' big governments collapse, we expect to see more and more people taking advantage of the end of national taxation tyranny and living offshore themselves. These locations will become the key places for the growing numbers of e-locals and niche-fund managers (not to mention niche bankers) to congregate. While the old *laissez-faire* City of London will still be a dealing hub in many respects, all regulated onshore financial centers will find themselves dwindling relative to the virtual world and electronic trading will take more and more markets offshore.

"The mindset of taxes is rooted in concepts such as atoms and place. With both of those more or less missing, the basics of taxation will have to change."
Nicholas Negroponte

Ten Offshore tips for the top, in alphabetical order:

- *Andorra* – Somewhat of an anarchists' paradise, Andorra is situated in the Pyrennees between France and Spain. Nowadays, with a firm banking regime in place and attractive tax-free packages available for residents, it is ideally placed to exploit the Capital Market Revolution.

- *Bermuda* – A highly wired location, close to the USA and with good infrastructure, Bermuda has everything, even its very own stockmarket. We expect parallel listings to explode on this offshore market if US regulators or stockmarket officials persist in behaving as if the world nations still operate in isolation from each other.

- *British Virgin Islands* – A key tax haven for offshore companies, these islands have one of the best jurisdictions for operating funds and fund-related businesses.

- *Canary Islands / Madeira* – The Spanish-ruled Canary Islands and the Portuguese colony of Madeira are vying to create an offshore haven in their respective regions. Both offer great potential if they can grasp the modalities of the New Reality.

- *Channel Islands* – Whilst it is difficult to get residency in these islands nevertheless they offer a very good base for banking. Sark looks especially promising given its lack of legal constraints.

- *Gibraltar* – Despite being dented by occasional struggles, the territory still benefits from its fringe-of-Europe location.

- *Hong Kong* – The interventions of the Hong Kong government to prop up the stock market in 1998 was a sad folly. Hopefully, the communists have learnt their lesson and will allow the Hong Kong property market to stay reasonably deflated.

- *Isle of Man* – A small island off the coast of the UK and Ireland, with a worldwide reputation for its offshore operations, the Isle of Man has an income tax at 20 per cent and no capital gains tax. We see it as the biggest winner amongst the British offshore islands, even though the Channel Islands are larger.

- *Monaco* – With a somewhat over-regulated economy, coupled to a bureaucratic and slow-moving government in a French imperial model, Monaco has certain drawbacks for state-of-the-art commerce. Nevertheless, the principality has the potential to explode. It is one of the most telephonically connected nations on Earth, and with judicious deregulation in the Singaporean mold, could become perhaps the most notable city state on the planet. We are very bullish about this nation provided it maintains reform of its executive to make it more business-friendly.

- *Singapore* – This city state of three million people has achieved incredible growth since independence and maintains an awesome reputation as one of the few global governments that maintains its pact with the electorate to keep streets clean, government functioning, and avoid overly burdening tax payers. The statist ethos of much of the state's bureaucracy is its current Achilles heel. However, the state's big bang reforms announced in May 1999 have considerable promise. Singapore managed to cope better than much of South-East Asia during the Asian economic meltdown in the late 1990s. Singapore right now is still too rigid in its economic structures: it needs to develop entrepreneurship and it needs to lose its obsession with only allowing big names in the financial world to play from its state-of-the-art digital city state. But in the new millennium the Singapore government seems to be taking to heart the need to deregulate, deregulate, and deregulate once more. If it can manage the transition from semi-planned corpocracy to a thriving entrepreneurial base then the prospects for Singapore, already a world-beating economy are simply awesome.

If they get their act together, a number of nations have great potential. Australia certainly has one of the best lifestyles on Earth, provided it rationalizes (whether as a federation or independent nations) its grinding bureaucracy and finds a way to raise government finance without squeezing tax rates to excessive levels on firms and individuals alike.

As long as the European Union appears blithely oblivious of global trends towards more socialism, there is little hope for any European nation maintaining a "third way" to prosperity in the information age. This is, as the *Far Eastern Economic Review* accurately described it a "Shangri-La" approach. However, with the rest of the

The key to prosperity in the Capital Market Revolution will be flexibility.

world breaking into ever smaller states – a process that is likely to occur within the European Union itself by the end of the first decade of the new millennium at the latest – the EU will either break up or be reduced to a regional trading block. The latter option could be preferable, rather than the EU continuing to set lofty and potentially disastrous harmonization policies from Brussels as it did in the 1980s and 1990s. Provided the Euro currency holds together, this may accelerate the process of economic liberalization that individual governments have been unable to countenance in the past.

The key to prosperity in the Capital Market Revolution will be flexibility. Larger countries could become as competitive as smaller states as soon as their governments implement radical policies that give residents tax rates that are commensurate with the level of services the government provides, rather than operating a monopoly that imposes taxation on workers the government feels it can control. In the information age, the smart money will be ever more flexible and movable.[1]

> "The most obvious benefits will flow to the 'cognitive elite,' who will increasingly operate outside political boundaries. They are already equally at home in Frankfurt, London, New York, Buenos Aires, Los Angeles, Tokyo, and Hong Kong. Incomes will become more unequal within jurisdictions and more equal between them."
>
> **James Dale Davidson and William Rees-Mogg, *The Sovereign Individual***

Alas, many governments will fail to seize opportunities. While it is the most distant locations that have the potential of the greatest gains, it will also be the most distant states that may have the greatest hurdles to overcome in becoming globally literate and capable of operating within a world-information framework. A glance at the letters page of a paper such as the *West Australian*, with massive circulation in its home state and a good grasp of world affairs, reveals just how many citizens still fear the privatization process. They see it robbing the family silver rather than realizing that, without such transition away from big government, the future prospects – even for an immensely mineral-rich area such as Western Australia – are hugely threatened.

Indeed, some executives will fail to get the plot even when the seeds of popular revolution are being sown on the streets. They will be unable to understand the dynamics of change in the information age. Such revolutionary change is never good for existing élites as they cannot truly hope to maintain their existing grasp on power. As it was for many introverted courts at the end of the fifteenth century when feudalism was breaking down, so it will also be true for the nanny states trying desperately to hold on to socialist principals of equivalence as the information age drives them bankrupt. Alas, this will affect a great many people who will find the safety nets of society far less available, if not withdrawn altogether. And refusing to accept the dynamic progress of the information age is not going to ensure that any of us avoids its consequences.

> "Governments can and will continue to intervene to try to influence foreign exchange rates and bond prices. But all they will be doing is creating anomalies from which participants in the market can profit. By definition, government intervention is an attempt to cause the market to establish a different price than the forces of supply and demand would otherwise dictate. When the stock of liquid financial assets was small and the market was far less integrated, government action (particularly when co-ordinated on a multi-lateral basis) could overwhelm the relatively weak market."
>
> **Lowell Bryan and Diana Farrell,** *Market Unbound*

Until your government appreciates the New Reality borne of the Capital Market Revolution, it will be an increasing danger to your wealth, health, and happiness, in the same way that a wasp is so lethal just as it is finally dying at the end of the summer season. Existing notions of statism passed through summer 30 years ago, their autumn has been a long and increasingly difficult one. Only a deathly winter now awaits them in the new millennium.

For many investors and traders in the New Reality, the pitfalls are huge – but the rewards are enormous.

Nevertheless, the burden of managing change lies with individuals too. Remember, only the swift and most flexible will survive. For many investors and traders in the New Reality, the pitfalls are huge – but the rewards are enormous.

Emerging cybermarkets will have a huge impact upon every citizen of the world who has assets in any form of financial, stock, bond, or commodity investment. Every private and publicly traded company, every employee in financial markets, every official in government will be affected for better or for worse, for richer or poorer, by the tidal change of information. Electronic trading will transform every global market, every government, and affect every strata of society. As *Business Week* magazine noted: "The changes will be both disruptive and liberating."

Towards a new capitalism

The existing food chains are dying. The new model of global business effectively undermines nation statehood. For those who think that manufacturing cannot be affected, one need look no further than the increasingly cut-throat business of government agencies the world over offering increasing subsidies and tax reliefs to anybody establishing manufacturing businesses on their terrain. Nations such as the Republic of Ireland[2] have used their grants and loans from the EU, as well as an aggressive marketing policy in industrial development, to build a hugely successful modern nation. Ireland boasts excellent global communications, a skilled workforce, and income levels that are now surpassing that of the UK. In the information age, the economics of a state come down to a micro level. Ireland is a perfect size for a new-age nation. Indeed its neighbor, Northern Ireland, with many similar benefits as the Republic in terms of workforce skill, may even be able to operate as a successful independent nation within the concepts of the information age – despite being saddled by an excessive public sector (a legacy of British government policy attempting to counteract the threat of terrorism). The twenty-first century will offer the people of Northern Ireland unparalleled opportunities to change their nation from an obscure province on the periphery of Europe into a global powerhouse at the center of the world. It happened before when Belfast was a leading industrial city during Britain's industrial revolution. If the government can grasp the concepts of the cyber age, Belfast can exceed the glories of its era as a center for shipbuilding and textiles when it was known as "Linenopolis." In the new millennia, any small state of five million people or less can place itself at the epicenter of the global economy.

Notes

1 As an indication of how one can keep working while on the move in the information age, *Capital Market Revolution* was written while travelling through Rome, Paris, Hong Kong, Barcelona, Geneva, Zurich, Sydney, Perth and Albany in Western Australia. Research visits included Ireland, Japan, Malaysia, Singapore, the UK, and the USA.

2 Ironically the EU appears to have stifled the Dublin International Financial Services Centre (IFSC) through requiring quotas for companies seeking to join the IFSC from 1999.

CHAPTER 8

The microbanking manifesto

How small can be beautiful too

> "A whole industry is shifting from the physical world to the virtual."
> **The Economist October 1998.**

As one walks across from the Bank of England in Threadneedle Street, London, one passes the incredible front of the Royal Exchange. Nowadays a magnificent Georgian structure, dealing operations have taken place at this site since the Middle Ages. More recently, the LIFFE futures market began within its beautiful shell. Approaching Mansion House as one crosses the end of Cornhill, the amazing history of the City of London is everywhere in evidence.

Crossing King William Street, and just beside the Mansion House – the magnificent ceremonial headquarters for the incumbent of that most famous of civic positions, the Lord Mayor of London – one reaches a rather anonymous-looking Georgian building. Inside "One Lombard Street" is a magnificent restaurant, occupying a wonderful banking hall long-since rendered redundant by the march of technology in the financial industry. In its heyday, this long white-walled chamber, complete with a domed ceiling that bathes the interior in natural light, was used by many great bankers of the Empire. Now the wheeler-dealers of the electronic age increasingly congregate for splendid dining within an austere yet magnificently charismatic environment.

Similar gastronomic ingenuity has transformed the likes of the former Reserve Bank of Australia Hall in Sydney's CBD into a fine dining restaurant that is appropriately titled "Banc." Throughout the world, banking rationalization and mergers have left many fine premises unoccupied. With the Capital Market Revolution driving staff numbers down, even these restaurants may ultimately find themselves forced out of business as financial districts struggle to come to terms with the stunning changes being wrought by the upheaval throughout capital markets. In the world of banking, retail and wholesale, the changes will be no less stunning.

> "The only matter of consequence silicon produces are relationships."
> **Kevin Kelly, Editor of *Wired***

The world of banking has been increasingly transfixed by the increasing merger mania at the very top end. To be a serious bank, one has to be a serious global player. To be a serious global player, one needs to be in as many physical locations as possible, not just for retail banking but for investment banking and related functions too. Global megabanks will probably reign supreme for a decade or more before a wave of New Reality rationalization befalls them. Meanwhile, the banks that will have the greatest effect upon the world at large will be a tiny fraction of the size of the megabanks. Microbanks will become the massive success story of the twenty-first century. They will be tiny institutions, with staffs smaller than most existing megabanks' IT departments. Yet such institutions will be global, with only token offices in more than one jurisdiction. They will be capable of handling vastly complex banking transactions from almost any part of the globe. They will exist almost entirely in cyberspace – virtual banks servicing a virtual world.

In the New Reality, any bank can operate anywhere, regardless of the banking statutes in force. Indeed, whereas the USA has often had a relatively open policy towards the creation of new banking insti-tutions, many European countries have traditionally been loath to accept new banks, unless they have staggering quantities of capital available. Some of the few new banks to be established in the UK during the 1990s were all owned by supermarket chains. The existing banking industry was incredulous that businesses skilled in stacking shelves, shuffling produce into a network of stores ahead of impending sell-buy dates, and providing a wide choice of consumer products for the customer, were intending to enter the "specialized" business of banking. The moral indignation of existing bankers at the government permitting such new competition only served to demonstrate just how mollycoddled banks had been and just how far away from reality the banking business had become.

A premium on incompetence

"Online banking puts further strain on the established clearing banks with their antiquated notions that it takes three days to clear a check – in an age of real-time, 24-hours-a-day, global transactions this simply will not do. Digital cash systems – micropayment schemes – will not only create the largest market in the world but also – because of the attraction of issuing proprietary digital cash – threaten the very foundation of established finance – and point towards a disintermediation of many of the financial institutions that have emerged since the industrial revolution – maybe even the disintermediation of national governments."

Bob Cotton, Paris Derivatives Exhibition, October 1998

Almost throughout the world, bankers are unpopular. Given their aloof, incompetent, uncommunicative ways of dealing with customers, it is not difficult to see why. Banks have had a lovely cartel for too long. If clients disliked being a captive client of one bank, they could switch to another and

Banks have had a lovely cartel for too long.

be treated with the same cavalier disregard. Banks knew that they were the only safe guardians of money and that their audience was essentially trapped into doing business with them. In other words, banks treated their customers with the same blithe disregard as governments treated their citizens. No matter how bad their service was, people would still need banks. With only limited competition in most jurisdictions, banks knew they could stay in business, thanks to the government restricting new banks entering the business.

The New Reality slices straight through the concept of existing banking procedure and will significantly undermine all the monopolistic advantages enjoyed by banks during the post-war era. In the information age banks will compete across borders – without recourse to local regulations. Some pensioners will stay onshore for the sake of maintaining greater banking safety (whether this is perceived or real will matter little to many of this constituency), but with banking regulations increasingly covering only minor quantities of deposits, individuals will see less and less advantage in keeping their transactions online.

Micropayment – the key to new banking

Banks traditionally make their money from fees charged for transactions, as, well as by holding money for periods of time during transactions when it is legally owned by a client. Such clearing services are increasingly farcical. Transactions beyond national borders are costly and frequently incompetent. The SWIFT system supposedly offers three-day transfers between the UK and Italian banks. In reality, the process can easily take a fortnight. When a customer tries to discover what has gone wrong, each bank shrugs its shoulders and points the finger of blame at the other. Even within domestic markets, lodging checks often means a three-day wait before the money is actually lodged in an account. In the information age, when other businesses are increasingly adjusting to improved information flow, the banks seem to be setting their computers to the task of making charges on transactions easier without adding any form of value to the service.

With the Capital Market Revolution already destabilizing financial market transactions, the core banking business of holding money and moving it from one place to another (a business at which banks appear singularly incompetent in many instances) will be revolutionized. Banks will no longer be able to expect fat fees for minuscule effort. In the information age the commoditization of banking will result in increased facility of

Banks will no longer be able to expect fat fees for minuscule effort.

transactions and remarkable drops in fees. Micropayments will be the norm for banking transactions. Transaction costs will drop to a few cents even for what is today regarded as a "sophisticated" cross-border wire transfer. Furthermore, transactions will be in real-time. Banks will lose the capacity to rape their clients through fees and the withholding of their funds. Unless they make massive adjustments to their overheads and dealing practices, correspondent banks will wither and die.

Using cybermoney, there will be a huge new market for tiny transactions. Microroyalties will be increasingly payable online for information. A single article from a newspaper will be purchasable for a few cents, and the bank will receive maybe as little as a fraction of a cent for facilitating the transaction. Increasingly, parallel forms of e-cash will compete for transaction dollars. Online, many currencies will be corporatized, owned by institutions with either the enabling technology such as Microsoft or the commercial reputation of a global brand, like McDonalds. Many micropayment schemes have been in trials ever since the RSA strong public-key encryption scheme became publicly available in 1995. Virtual cash will become the currency oiling the world's economy and its financial markets in the aftermath of the Capital Market Revolution.

The analysts Frost and Sullivan calculated relative costs of simple cash withdrawals in 1998 showing how e-cash is destined to beat the banks (all costs are in US dollars):

Personal over-the-counter transactions   1.95
ATM transactions   0.80
Telephone banking transactions   0.60

Internet banking transactions	0.30
Internet credit card transactions	0.20
E-cash transactions	0.01

Source: Frost & Sullivan Telecoms newsletter, March 1998.

New currencies

E-cash will be the money of the future. Alas, governments think that by more transactions becoming electronic, they can control more of their citizens' desires to move money around and therefore plug holes in the increasingly damaged nets they use to trawl the world looking for tax avoidance and evasion. They will be proven wrong, not just because of the quantity of the transactions, which will swamp their ability to monitor them, but also because the banks will increasingly operate beyond their remit.

Banks will predominantly be based offshore. They may even operate in parallel locations to stop predatory policing by increasingly desperate large nations. Dale Davidson and Rees-Mogg neatly described how an investor will place all assets "in a cyberaccount in a cyberbank that is domiciled simultaneously in Newfoundland, the Cayman Islands, Uruguay, Argentina, and Liechtenstein. If any of the jurisdictions attempt to withdraw operating authority or seize the assets of depositors, the assets will automatically be transferred to another jurisdiction at the speed of light."[1]

E-cash will not merely be equivalent to existing currencies such as the US dollar or Japanese Yen; increasingly it will take on a life of its own and indeed will ultimately subsume many, if not all, national currencies.

The end of Fiat money?

"A more advanced stage will mark the transition to true cybercommerce. Not only will transactions occur over the Net, but they will migrate outside the jurisdiction of nation-states. Payment will be rendered in cyber-currency. Profits will be booked in cyberbanks. Investments will be made in cyberbrokerages. Many transactions will not be subject to taxation. At this stage, cybercommerce will begin to have significant megapolitical consequences of the kind we have already outlined. The powers of government over traditional areas of the economy will be transformed by the new logic of the Net. Extraterritorial regulatory power will collapse. Jurisdictions will devolve. The structure of firms will change, and so will the nature of work and employment.

This outline of the stages of the information revolution is only the barest sketch of what could be the most far-reaching economic transformation ever."

James Dale Davidson and William Rees-Mogg, *The Sovereign Individual*

Of course, investors will need an incentive to invest in such digital money. Initially, consumers will hold small quantities of virtual cash in order to facilitate online transactions. However, as the virtual world develops, the prevalence of online transactions will increasingly encourage investors to move more money online. Increasingly desperate attempts by governments to clamp down on assets left onshore will only serve to accelerate the process. In the end, the best stores of value will win.

> **We believe the currency of the future will be asset-backed.**

Like all market structures, a wide array of currencies will exist in cyberspace, although only a small number will gain widespread acceptance. We believe the currency of the future will be asset-backed. One of the more frightening aspects of the finances of the late twentieth century has been the common use of worthless "Fiat" money. A financial crisis in the future will make the worthlessness of "Fiat" money operated by increasingly out-of-touch governments all the more apparent. In the future, currencies will revert to being asset-backed. Digital cash will equate to quantities of silver or gold and other precious metals.

Interestingly, no less an economist than Freidrich von Hayek argued as long ago as 1976 that the implementation of competing private currencies would be an effective weapon in reducing, if not entirely eliminating, inflation.[2] Privately issued money must retain its value or investors will be attracted to a currency that can safely maintain its valuation. In the information age, digital money issued by a wide range of organizations on a huge number of premises will increasingly bring Hayek's dream to reality. Indeed, since 1990 there have been decreasing costs of operation in all areas of information technology.

Money will increasingly take on other characteristics too. With increasing commoditization of financial processes it will be perfectly feasible to use a vast array of fungible versions of electronic trans-action units (ETUs) which will take an infinite number of forms. ETUs will be limited in their construction only by the ingenuity of humans to develop them. In a wired world where real-time valuation is a fact of life, anything can be instantly traded. Use of ETUs may be dismissed as barter by governments, but increasingly it will be impossible to discern what is really money and what an asset. In the online world, real-time valuation makes all assets instantly transferable.

In a wired world where real-time valuation is a fact of life, anything can be instantly traded.

Typical early examples of ETUs will probably include equity-linked money where the cash is collateralized by share values. Such cash will be backed by the assets of a company and valued as a function of the stock price. Instead of having to sell stock, the online consumer will be able instantly to buy household goods, or a car, or property online, with payment in stock notes. Vendors will be able instantly to transfer the value of the ETU into the digital cash of their choice (for a minuscule transaction fee) or hold the ETU in its current form. Of course, such quasi-barter may not appeal to tax authorities, but then again the virtual world will remain an ostensibly tax-free zone. Taxes will accrue according to the juris-diction in which an individual or a company wishes to locate.

Other forms of ETU will include securitized notes based on bank-loan portfolios, or mortgages, or insurance policies – or any form of financial asset. Ultimately, the realms of ETUs are limited only by the imagination. We expect that there will be ETUs based on such relatively esoteric concepts as the success of football clubs. In what more imaginative a way could soccer fans be invited to fund their football team's new stadium or player acquisitions than by inviting them to buy discounted ETUs which rise as the club gains points in the league or wins domestic or international competitions?

In the old days, companies and sports clubs had to issue bonds through complex offering-memoranda governed by securities laws. In the New Reality, bonds will become ETUs. ETUs will be essentially cash (thanks to instantaneous 24-hour-a-day valuation on electronic markets) and will be readily transferable for goods and services in a way that has not been seen for several centuries. In the future the whole business of money will become a part of our everyday lives. The cybertraders and e-locals who go online early in the revolution will be well placed to capitalize on the enormous change in business, commerce, and domestic lifestyle.

Governments lose more power

As governments find themselves increasingly pushed out of the monopoly provision of currency issuance, they will doubtless endeavor to destroy the early forms of digital cash and ETUs threatening their existence. Alas, it will be too late. Cries of anguish that the whole system is unregulated by government intervention will be true. The inference that the system is more dangerous as a result will be false. After all, banking systems have often flourished without government intervention or the questionable benefits of government guarantees on deposits (which throughout history have tended to become little more than a government charter to foster banking inefficiency or excessive risk taking). Private currencies competed successfully in Scotland for much of the first half of the eighteenth century without any form of Scottish central bank. Private bankers (free to enter the market) took deposits while issuing their own currency backed by gold bullion.

> "There was little fraud. There was no evidence of over-issue of notes. Banks did not typically hold either excessive or inadequate reserves. Bank runs were rare and not contagious. The free banks commanded the respect of citizens and provided a sound foundation for economic growth that outpaced that in England for most of the period."
>
> **Michael Prowse, *Financial Times*, 5 February 1996**

Microbankers will encompass a whole new league of small-scale private banks and investment banking operations – somewhat similar to the vast number of firms established in the nineteenth century. Their unique brand of direct capitalism threatens to undermine entirely most of the attempts of rich governments to regulate markets during the past fifty years. In the nineteenth century, comparatively small banking institutions such as Barings, Lazards, and Rothschilds were able to lend monies across the globe, both within and beyond the broad control of the British Empire. Banking will in many ways return to this sort of relationship in the new millennium. Banks will be able to handle millions, even billions in deposits, transactions, and loans, with only a

Banks will be able to handle millions, even billions in deposits, transactions, and loans, with only a minuscule number of staff.

minuscule number of staff. Once again, the established interests have a huge amount to fear from the Capital Market Revolution as nimble new players will be able to run rings around their massive bureaucracies. With public key encryption (as used for instance in ATM transactions at large commercial entities) now commonplace, the advantage is increasingly shifting in favor of the cyberbankers and cyberfinanciers. Established onshore banks will become little more than facilitators of mortgages for onshore investment and owners of ATM machine networks for those few transactions that actually require paper money. Indeed, physical cash coins and notes will be largely defunct by 2020.

Meanwhile, the cyberbankers in the new era will be faced with the wonderful opportunity of providing a global service to customers throughout the world from the comfort of tiny offshore offices (perhaps several in parallel). The offshore regimes that offer the best terms for banking licences will swiftly tap into a hugely profitable market as more and more companies congregate in offshore banking colonies. Whilst there may still be token offices in the old world's financial centers such as London, New York, or Tokyo, for appearances sake, the future banking centers of the world will be city states like Bermuda or Singapore.

> "Moreover, the implications of one industry's changes go far beyond its boundaries. As financial firms discover and improve new ways of conducting commerce, their efforts will spread across entire economies."
>
> **The Economist**

A microbanker's blueprint

In the New Reality, small is beautiful. Exquisitely beautiful. In the past it was thought a hindrance to be small because it showed a palpable lack of capital and a lack of global orientation. Smart money tended to migrate to the big institutions where "one-stop" shopping was feasible and a viewpoint on just about any region of the world was reasonably possible.

Nowadays, the modern investment bank can be a genuine "microbank." An organization has no need to spatter the world with branches or representative offices in order to establish its global credentials. Staff costs can be minimal as retained staff numbers are exceptionally modest. Through judicious use of "e-lancers" and new technology, the modern electronic brokerage and its micro-investment banking capability will be able to flourish within small and large local, regional, continental, and even global niches.

By using outsourced services, the new model investment banking operation can outpace its competitors and offer global services for all forms of brokerage operations while also avoiding excessive regulatory costs. Unless the established G7 nations

▶

change their act, the classic modern brokerage will not be found in the USA, the UK, or any other European country if socialist plans for tax harmonization take place.

The new-model brokerage is likely to be headquartered offshore. Central financial district rents are too high, localized regulation too cumbersome, and the perils of withholding taxation simply too much red tape for microbrokers. With the institutional microbrokers, there will be regional representatives, probably working on a contract basis (and not necessarily full time) in a series of offshore locations close to the major client areas in both time and distance. Some microbrokers will stay onshore to service those superannuation funds and big banks who will remain in city-center financial districts for some years to come. There will be a comprehensive service available to all major global exchanges, quite possibly for a variety of markets – stocks, cash bonds, and derivatives products – and all available from a single terminal. Depending on the size of the client, access to the central servers could be by direct ISDN line or an Internet connection. All clearing services will be handled by a top-grade custodian bank who will hold all funds for the broker, thus negating credit concerns for clients placing money with these brokers.

Exchange "memberships" (or at least access permits) may still fall to those brokers operating locally and microbrokers will simply be happy to pay a marginal premium to the exchange permit holders for the privilege of dealing on particular markets. However, if the premium is perceived to be too great then business will migrate to another exchange. After all, that is precisely the New Reality encapsulated within the Capital Market Revolution.

On the banking front, a microbank may choose to offer solely investment banking services. However, many will also be able to secure offshore deposit licences, which will help to enrich many an offshore island looking to upgrade its living standards by embracing digital finance. In addition to deposit-taking, the new microbankers will offer a full suite of specialist investment banking services. This will include stock-market listing (probably on the most competitive new offshore exchanges) and perhaps ultimately Direct Public Offerings as well. It will be possible to transact all business through the Internet. Meanwhile, the bank will have its own underwriting services available (probably using private capital rather than large institutional money which traditionally demands relatively extortionate returns). The funds management arm of the microbanks will contain a vast global capacity for managing innovative and dynamic assets. Again, only a handful of people will be required to maintain billions of dollars in assets. The assets themselves will probably be ring-fenced in a completely separate offshore jurisdiction to the bank itself, to ensure complete protection for investors. Needless to say, it will be possible to review all asset management services on the microbank's secure Internet site.

The bank's deal-making corporate finance teams will actually work as consultants to a series of institutions for different projects, working on a particular deal as and when it is happening close to their geographic locale. The bank will also have a good research department. Perhaps the technical analyst will have been in Western Australia for some years, while the economists may all come from Mumbai, an excellent source of relatively cheap but highly-educated analysis compared to the hideous salary multiples expected by American MBAs. In the seamless world of digital communication, the bank's research staff will all appear as a homogenous entity, even though several will never even have visited the bank's offshore headquarters. Moreover they will all be paid in some way by results. Meanwhile, the bank's team of brokers, who cover all the world's equity, bond, and derivatives markets, will be regularly traveling the world liaising with clients while monitoring client positions on their laptops.

Of course, in the old days, to operate such a global multinational bank would have required millions of dollars in overheads alone. Now this microbank can be a leviathan amongst the tiny banks and still manage to issue securities, advise on mergers, provide stock and derivative brokerage throughout the world, offer extensive fund management solutions as well as its own proprietary trading activities – and all with a mere 30 staff.

The venture capital revolution

"Clamour from small investors who want venture capital returns will alter how companies fund themselves, and perhaps alter the nature of ownership."

The Economist

In the past venture capital has been a curious business – a bureaucratic operation with its own conventions. Venture capitalists typically tend to seek so much equity for the financing they inject that they are routinely referred to as "vulture capitalists." Outside the USA they command little respect, although firms such as the British-based 3i have been very successful. It is the American culture that has allowed successful venture management – in Europe too many organizations balk at the initial sums of money required and fail to see the potential upside. Essentially the USA is simply more entrepreneurial. In Europe a failed idea can lead to venture-capital ostracism; in the USA there is no indignity in a failed venture for either party. Indeed, such has been the culture of capitalism in the USA that in California some legal and other service firms have become rich on investments in companies as a *pro bono* for services rendered. In Europe, accountancy and law firm partners tend to go weak at the very thought of giving up income for any form of investment.

Nevertheless, in Europe and indeed anywhere beyond the more freewheeling and dealing shores of the USA, the whole concept of venture capital has been one that has largely failed to make a major impact. One cannot blame existing venture capitalists for their desire to cherry-pick the best deals. However, at the same time, many projects have floundered or have been severely constrained by the relative lack of venture-capital funding available. The Capital Market Revolution will change all this. The revolution may not destroy existing businesses (indeed they may even prosper without the kind of radical changes to their current structures that their banking and broking brethren will have to make). Nevertheless, the opportunities afforded by the Capital Market Revolution will be enormous. New businesses will be able to find funding and existing businesses will be able to expand in a way unprecedented since the Industrial Revolution.

With traders increasingly able to take control of their own destiny and with the Internet reducing the cost of accessing capital, the entire venture-capital industry will see its core markets made much more competitive as companies increasingly use new, cheaper middlemen (or even go directly online under their own auspices) to raise capital. The key to this whole aspect of the revolution will be the increasing commoditization and globalization of investment and industrial/business markets. New pools will spring up to invest in technology or other specialist applications companies across the globe. The trading in the after-market of shares and holdings in small companies will be radically amended. Such dealing will be risky but the rewards will be vast.

In the new era, the smart venture capitalists will be online. They will not require huge numbers of employees to monitor investment opportunities, since a great deal of the work will be contracted out to third-party specialists, working in geography, industry sector, and other appropriate niches. The whole process of seeking investment for business will be greatly facilitated by being able to go online to seek out a venture-capital broker who can offer a business the best service to help it expand, survive, and prosper in the New Reality. The use of contemporary multimedia for presentations will radically help promote business throughout the world and will help entrepreneurs find finance without having to waste tedious amounts of time traveling between presentations in city offices.

> In the new era, the smart venture capitalists will be online.

Increasing globalization will permit ever simpler valuation of companies according to industry sector (although some small regional disparities may remain). However, the more business is transacted in cyberspace, the more such companies will be valued on the same premises.

Contemporary venture capital is a mix of specialist funds and its processes will increase alongside the growth of funds – as outlined in Chapter 6. In future, venture capital funding through networks of interested parties will be online. At present, such networks tend to be heavily localized, but soon they will be global. Pools of investors may be ready to invest in projects at the click of a mouse, hugely speeding up the whole venture-capital process. For entrepreneurs, the entire process will be a godsend.

The disintermediation process will permit more and more entrepreneurs to go directly online to seek the funding they require. The modern venture capitalists will probably cluster around their Web sites, which have built up a reputation for quality deals. Their fees will be much lower than currently sought by many investment banks, even presuming such banks would actually organize the funding in the first place. With margins for organizing funding under threat, only the swift will survive. Having said that, the prospect for those venture capitalists who can adapt to the New Reality are, as ever, enormous. With an increasing number of professional investors drawn from the ranks of e-locals and those retired and prematurely retired, the pool available for direct venture capital investment will grow significantly – even if it is only tiny in relation to the overall size of investment funds available to these groups.

Notes

1 James Dale Davidson and William Rees-Mogg, *The Sovereign Individual*.
2 Freidrich von Hayek, *The Denationalisation of Money*.

CHAPTER 9

Living with the revolution

How you can survive and profit in turbulent times

> "As we enter the twenty-first century – a century in which machines will conjure up and process information in essentially limitless quantities – what will retain value, both personally and professionally, is what computers cannot produce: that most intangible and elusive of economic goods, but actually the one with the most enduring value – the creative output of the human mind. This is still – in the economist's terminology as well as in common parlance – a scarce resource ."
>
> **Dr. Charles Jonscher, President of the Central Europe Trust Company**
> **(from Anne Leer, *Masters of the Wired World*)**

The Capital Market Revolution is likely to become a huge destroyer of jobs. As is typical of all revolutions, existing interests will suffer. For those who are currently employed within and around the securities industry, the risks posed by the Capital Market Revolution are massive. At the same time, the benefits for those well placed will be quite stunning. Nevertheless, all practitioners will need to make some sacrifices, or at least amendments to their lifestyle, if they are to succeed in the information age.

Listed below are the five key areas of change which we believe will help existing financial players to achieve continued job stability (presuming of course that they don't wish to start their own operation to take advantage of the New Reality).

Survival skills for the revolution

- *Computer literacy* – If you don't have this you're history. If you want to get it, there are hundreds of courses available in night schools the world over. Learn how to use the major spreadsheets, word processors, and other applications. Try to learn a little about programming. Even if you never actually program anything, you will at least understand a bit about the dynamics of programming. Remember that support jobs and management/IT liaison will be growth areas in the New Reality. Similarly, the use of the Internet will not just be important to future financial dealings, it will be pivotal.

- *Language skills* – It will soon be possible to speak Mandarin at the touch of a button during a telephone call, thanks to an online translator. Despite this, Naisbitt's "Global Paradox" principle that the more global things become, the more the influence of the individual increases – will still apply. Skilled abilities in foreign languages will remain prized assets for financial practitioners – especially as the NewVas broker is likely to spend considerable amounts of time traveling to clients in their home countries.

- *Geographical flexibility* – In the New Reality nobody can continue to expect to work in New York and live upstate in the commuter belt. The best jobs will often be in foreign countries – and frequently offshore ones at that. Employees who limit their home to a narrow geographical area (even one so globally relevant and cosmopolitan as New York or London) will find their prospects severely diminished.

- *Market knowledge* – We foresee stockbrokers being amongst the least employable of those made redundant after the Capital Market Revolution. Why? Because they have the narrowest focus of any major brokerage group. They tend only to understand how to sell securities within narrow fields (in the new globalized market even the whole American stock market is a narrow field compared to the vast array of investment opportunities soon to be found at one-stop shops online). In the futures markets, while a large number of relatively narrowly-focused, execution-oriented brokers remain, their days are numbered. Remember, the people who succeed in the information age will become a cognitive élite. The brokers who succeed will be an informed, globally literate, cognitive élite.

- *Global thinking* – The virtual world is one in which the entire market will be available at the click of a mouse. Specialization in one narrow, locally-focused sector is already insufficient to maintain employment at many leading institutions. Brokers, analysts, and traders need to think macro, with an eye on the micro, when it comes to research and trading. The old concept of simply trading a particular share because it holds a niche in one small national market is over. In the future, the market will be more niche-bound than ever, but those niches will be regional and global, rather than provincial.

The new markets

There will be many new markets to which specialists will be attracted. As ever, there will be a shortage of practitioners to fill vacancies, so the first in will often reap significant benefits (when LIFFE opened in 1982, many previously passed-over middle managers made a killing by running initially tiny floor teams and being carried along with the growth of the market).

In addition to the many opportunities we have already outlined for those who can find a niche in funds management and banking operations, listed below are the big growth areas for new product which we foresee in the near future:

- *Weather* – Derivatives based on weather are an interesting proposition for everybody from insurers through to event organizers and any corporation that may be troubled by excessive weather conditions. We expect weather trading to be enormous by the end of the first decade of the new millennium. Already OTC transac-

183

tions have been taking place since the late 1990s and it seems likely that exchange contracts will be commonplace by 2005.

- *Electricity* – A nascent market but, when combined with oil and other energy products and linked to weather derivatives, one that has enormous potential. Power producers and large industrial consumers will convert this market into a multi-billion dollar environment by early in the new century.

- *Credit* – The emergence of credit derivatives in the mid-1990s was a revolutionary force in the business of risk management. We expect an increasing move towards cleared credit derivatives of both OTC and exchange-traded contracts by 2005 (so removing the theoretically minuscule but nonetheless tricky stumbling block of counterparty risk in the guaranteeing of a separate counterparty risk!).

- *Emissions* – These are the final links in the chain connecting all forms of energy, along with weather and financial products, to the by-products of the industrial age. Emissions trading has been slow to build momentum because of the machinations of the bureaucrats at the various Earth Summits. However, with governments increasingly impotent in so many other ways, and with emissions being a global problem, we expect that market solutions will be seen as the most efficient means by far, rather than relying on government subsidy (which governments will increasingly find impossible to resource).

- *Insurance* – Linked with weather, we see insurance as a huge growth business. The insurance industry itself is likely to become more open to niche companies underwriting specific specialist policies, and this should enhance competition and create lower premiums for many policyholders. In addition, the use of insurance derivatives will increase the exchangeability of insurance policies, so leading to much lower prices for purchasers, as well as the likelihood of insurance products reaching a more consumerist audience through cheaper, simpler policies.

- *Islamic Finance* – With the growing importance of the Moslem world, the prospects for Islamic finance are increasing rapidly. Interpretation of this financial genre tends to differ from country to country (Malaysia for instance interprets Islamic finance differently from some more fundamentalist members of the Arab world). Nevertheless, Islamic finance will continue to grow in importance, a process which will be accelerated if the Moslem world comes closer to harmonizing its financial practices.

- *Securitization* – A moderate niche for many years, this process has come of age in Europe and the USA during the 1990s. With capital adequacy requirements to be met, many banks have found it easier to take loans off their balance sheets through securitized bond issues (on just about anything – car loans, mortgages, credit card receivables). Equally, there have been securitizations of properties and even pop star royalties (such as David Bowie). With increasing commoditization of securities markets and the greater facility for packaging such products in ever smaller quantities cost-effectively, we see securitization as a big growth area. Microbanks will become massive users of securitization processes, so as to maintain their modest staff size and flexibility of management, thus accelerating the securitization process further.

> In the New Reality the flexibility of derivatives products will be increasingly popular for investors, traders, and hedgers.

- *Telecommunications* – This already has fledgling markets, such as Band-X, which has been operated by Richard Elliott and Marcus de Ferranti from a nineteenth-century house near London's Victoria and Albert Museum since July 1997. Since telecommunications provide the oil that lubricates the information revolution, the prospects for traded cash and futures markets based around telephone lines are simply enormous.

There are also many other potential areas for growth. Like those listed above, they will be heavily reliant on trading in derivatives products. While there are many sadly misinformed Luddites who seem to believe that derivatives magically create risk, it will increasingly become good business practice to employ derivatives. In the 1990s millions of people in the developed world benefited from stable mortgage rates fixed for months and even years in advance, thanks to smart use of derivatives products by banks.

In the New Reality the flexibility of derivatives products will be increasingly popular for investors, traders, and hedgers. There will be many areas of large growth in existing products – we especially like the look of stock-related products as private share owners become increasingly sophisticated in their quest for maximizing returns. Equally, if food-oriented protectionism and subsidization can be broken down, then new and exciting commodity markets look likely. Potentially the biggest is rice, but at present the market is fragmented and overly protected by government regulation in big producer-nations such as Japan, precluding a global contract, although some regional trading takes place in the USA.

While we expect the largest financial marketplaces to become increasingly unified over the next decade, there will be a flowering of tiny niche market exchanges covering very narrow product lines. Thanks to the low cost of creating an online exchange mechanism, these exchanges will be created in increasing numbers. Likely markets will include such diverse markets as PC chips, fine wine, and essentially any other product whose price provides sufficient volatility as to interest speculators and attract hedgers looking to gain price stability.

Similarly, we believe the online gambling industry will increasingly overlap with the trading business. The hedging of political risks using "spread betting" (essentially a price system rather than a direct odds basis) will be attractive to many corporations and bankers. From here it is only a short move to have certain niche institutions taking a more active interest in the life-blood of spread-betting services such as sports events. Indeed, we expect that a major clearing house will soon be involved in the business of clearing spread-betting transactions to reduce risks by 2002 at the latest. In addition, the increasing commoditization of many areas of business will lead to clearing houses becoming much more actively involved in legal processes which require some form of fiduciary oversight. For instance, in Australia at least one clearing house has begun work on clearing residential property transactions. When such cash transactions can be expedited through a clearing house, the potential for some form of marketplace transaction system will be within sight. In this respect, disintermediation based on financial technology can lead to a new form of intermediation, albeit one that is much cheaper than the outmoded bureaucratic alternatives. Niche micromarkets will be a huge business by 2010, as evidenced by the growth of the online auction markets such as E-Bay in the early stages of the Internet's growth explosion.

> **For every NewVas broker in 2005, we believe at least 20 brokers will be unemployed.**

The job for me

The NewVas brokers who succeed will be hugely successful. However, it will be a tough market to enter. For every NewVas broker in 2005, we believe at least 20 brokers will be unemployed. Similarly, management in institutions will be severely slimmed, as the NewVas legacy coupled to the New Reality reaps havoc with existing management structure. Back offices will be massively restructured as the weight of paperwork from settlements continues to decline in all areas of trading. Increasing commoditization will make new product issuance simpler, thus helping securitization processes. Equally, the management and facilitation of ETUs will be a big growth area. The more mathematically inclined will find themselves actively occupied in the concept and design of creating ever more interesting ETU methods.

Information technology management and liaison will become ever more vital. The liaison function will be crucial, as brokers and all members of the food chain will need a greater understanding of each other's function. The German-Swiss EUREX exchange was not the first market to suffer poor liaison during the Capital Market Revolution – and it won't be the last.

In the New Reality, brokerage and regulatory jobs will be decimated. Exchanges are already laying off vast numbers of staff. The positions within clearing-houses are mostly filled already, although there may be some new clearing house operations in the near future. Indeed, telecommunications and other data provision companies may start muscling in on the exchange/clearing house provision market in an attempt to secure their revenues. If so, again liaison and management functions will be most in demand.

Retail financial services looks increasingly like a blood bath. However badly the banking unions feel their staff may have been treated in recent years, they really have seen nothing yet. Meanwhile, the sales of products such as insurance and mortgages look increasingly likely to migrate online. In this case, staff opportunities will be minimal, and existing employees will be culled *en masse*. In the area of financial planning, while services will again be migrating to the Internet, the prospects for another cognitive élite of NewVas brokers will arise. Here, the sales staff who manage to broaden their skills will find their success growing exponentially.

Risk management will remain a stable for employment in the securities business. We believe a successor to the existing JP Morgan VaR methodology (whose flaws, much documented elsewhere, we won't explore here)[1] will emerge before 2005. This will be a more dynamic, all-encompassing discipline. In fact as computer power continues to increase and with more and more traders operating from distant locations to their clearing agents or corporate headquarters, the business of online risk management will continue to expand in breadth and scope.

Even with the explosive growth of computer trading and Internet usage, the software business is likely to sustain its current critical mass. However, the opportunities are unlikely to be as plentiful as in ostensibly greenfield areas such as weather trading – the markets' growth surge has already happened, in the late 1980s and 1990s.

Meanwhile, the data business does not look overly healthy. With internet-based vendors able to offer cheaper and cheaper sources of supply, there will be tough times ahead for all but the most flexible of existing data suppliers. Job opportunities here look relatively narrow.

The simple facts of the Capital Market Revolution are that the changes will largely follow Pareto's Law. This states that 80 percent of the benefits accrue to 20 percent of those involved. This may actually prove to be overly optimistic. It is quite plausible that less than 10 percent of practitioners will gain 80 percent of the benefits between them. The winners in the Capital Market Revolution will be the most agile, creative, and diligent amongst the existing workforce. The cognitive and cyber élites will receive greater rewards than have been seen during the twentieth century for all but a handful of players. Life will be harder for those who

> **The winners in the Capital Market Revolution will be the most agile, creative, and diligent amongst the existing workforce.**

cannot be flexible in their residence or feel locked into a particular lifestyle. The Capital Market Revolution began by forcing change on the large institutions; it will conclude by ensuring that embracing change become the watchwords of the new trading élite.

Notes

1 To be fair to JPM and VaR, the problems of Value at Risk are more due to endusers believing the methodology was a cure-all rather than any deficiency per se in what remains a praiseworthy concept within limited applications.

Can global recession kill the cyber élite?

"There is nothing permanent except change."

Heraclitus

Many believe there is a new paradigm in the world of economics, created by a computerized information revolution, which is a supremely virtuous circle of growth, growth, and more growth. Alas, such suggestions are merely wrong, wrong, and wrong. Recessions will continue to come and go, blotting the economic landscape for many. However, traders in the New Reality who are suitably swift will of course be able to take advantage of any form of economic conditions. Those who merely acquire Internet-related stocks and hope to hang on for infinite games are playing a deadly game of "greater fool" theory. Similarly, volatility in financial markets will continue to provide boom-and-bust cycles. In some respects the increasing use of electronic methods may encourage greater volatility as e-locals become used to having to hit bids and lift offers to trade, rather than being able to play the bid/offer spread as they could when the cream of open-outcry trading was available to them.

One theory that is popular amongst some areas of society (for whom the term Luddite is only moderately harsh) is that the entire information revolution could be halted by a drastic recessions or even a depression – in a scenario similar to that following the 1929 Wall Street crash. But this is to misunderstand the entire nature of the information revolution. In the case of capital markets, future recession may only serve to accelerate the process of the New Reality. Faced with declining income, and worsening economic fundamentals, the very underpinnings of the industry will start to come adrift. Brokers and investment bankers will be forced to scythe costs. Those who have not openly embraced the New Reality will be bankrupted. With the costs of capital for participants in the cyber-banking and cybersecurities markets so much lower, opportunities to operate will be much simpler. With the revolution now irrevocably under way, there is simply nothing that can be done to stop it ripping the heart from the current financial establishment.

There will be hiccoughs along the road, in the same way that all revolutions are challenged, but although the revolution may be slowed down, it is bound to carry on unabated. There will be forks in the road, junctions to give way at, but overall the process will be unrelenting. New entrants who have missed the preliminary wave will have good opportunities to take part as shocks affect the system, but there will be no serious challenge to the cyber élite. Recession may slow the cyber élite down but nothing can now prevent their long-term accession to the control of capital markets. The future of financial markets is online.

In fact, there is nothing that can now stop the Capital Market Revolution from unfolding, apart from a nuclear holocaust destroying the world itself. The new, much more level playing field has already been laid, through the existing technological infra-structure of the Internet. As bandwidth multiplies on the World Wide Web during the next few years, the playing field will only become a neater, smoother pitch on which private capital will be able to play an essentially fair game against the institutions whose "masters-of-the universe" status looked impenetrable a mere handful of years ago.

Open outcry may survive for a few more years in centers such as Chicago, New York, and in a few isolated agricultural markets. However, it is to all intents and purposes dead. Indeed, if the Chicago and New York exchanges fail to get their act together very soon (expediting a major U-turn of their avowed policy for over a hundred years) then they, too, face oblivion. The core maxim of the New Reality ("no one person or party's place in the trading chain is now assured") will come back to haunt many existing large institutions. The businesses of "full service" stockbrokerage and funds management is likely to be decimated by smaller, more nimble organizations, capable of actively managing hundreds of millions and even billions of dollars within tiny management frameworks (similar to terrorist cells in the their tiny size but huge potential impact). These microbanks will use far more innovative methods than the large lumbering leviathans of the mutual fund business, who will find themselves hamstrung by being too large for the markets in which they operate. While a few bulge-bracket banks will survive, the biggest institutional fund managers look as doomed as dinosaurs.

The microbankers will threaten every facet of existing commercial and investment banking organizations' operations, armed with the new microcost processes of smart cards which will turn banking profits on their head. The use of smart cards providing ETU's – currency that actually has some value underpinning it – will leave government-issued money as a minority-holding for the public by 2010. Thanks to the new meritocracy, the cybertrading élite of e-locals and institutional dealers (often at microbanks) will enjoy vast rewards, even if the world economy does plunge into recession early in the new millennium. The rewards for being online remain enormous. The rewards for being an online financier as the Capital Market Revolution takes hold will be simply sensational.

Regulators have been used to acting like government – a monopoly provider in a finite landmass of the nation-state. Alas, they are ill-prepared to cope with the dynamics of the Capital Market Revolution, even if they understood what the New Reality is all about. Their future is bleak. As a result, markets will become more free-market and less subject to governmental whim. A new spirit of *caveat emptor* will permeate financial markets, which will increasingly operate offshore beyond the influence of government.

While we do believe that clearing houses will not have things quite as easy as they might expect (due to increased collateralization procedures on the OTC markets, etc.), nevertheless, their prospects significantly outshine those of the exchanges. The London Clearing

House (LCH), the leading independent clearing organization in the world and inextricably linked to one market or another, has a glorious future. The LCH is in an ideal position to create a global clearing house for all types of equity, financial, and commodity markets – and the sooner it is achieved, the easier it will be for traders to enjoy complete fungibility of trades across a wide range of asset classes, so potentially enhancing market liquidity.

Nevertheless, clearing houses, like exchanges, will have to be aware of the need to be very sensitive to public calls for openness when it comes to any trading accidents, errors or crises. The Salomons "big swinging elbow" affair almost destroyed the MATIF. The EUREX exchange may be beginning the new millenium as the largest market in Europe, but it must reform its clearing process (making it more open to new members) and also be aware of the prospects of being torpedoed by a resurgent LIFFE. The most successful exchanges in the future require not just an open dealing platform, they must also employ an open clearing system. In that respect, EUREX looks isolated. Finally, open public relations are vital to all exchanges with any activity related to screen dealing. Poor PR in a crisis will fatally damage an exchange.

On a personal note, we urge readers not to overly leverage themselves with city-center residential or business property in the boom financial cities of the late 1990s. The increasing movement of dealers away from CBD areas will inflict a massive bear market upon property prices, affecting not just residential real estate but also office and retail space as well. In London and New York especially, residential property prices will be catastrophically hit by the Capital Market Revolution. For employees, concerned about the revolution and its effects on their careers, we hope we have provided useful survival tips not only for living through the upheaval but also profiting from it. There will be massive job losses in financial markets – swingeing cuts are already in progress in several centers. Nevertheless, the opportunities arising from the Capital Market Revolution will be utterly enormous.

"While we're talking, envious time is fleeing; seize the day, put no trust in the future."

Horace

The physical network of financial market dealers has given way to the virtual. To remain still is to await death by a thousand cuts.

The shape of things to come

By Steve Black

Chuck stretched his arms above his head, dropped them back into his lap, and grunted with satisfaction. Life was good, he thought, as he gulped at his first coffee of the day. Glancing out of the window, he could just make out the shapes of the ducks on the nearest island on his lake. They too were beginning to stir in the gray streaks of light that signaled the approaching dawn.

This is the life. Sure beats the hell out of the 5.23, he thought, letting his mind drift back to the days of shivering on the first train into the city each morning.

Another gulp of coffee helped drag him back to the present. No need for that any more. Not now the world was properly wired. Everyone could work from wherever they wanted. It was a real win–win–win situation, he mused. The bank certainly won, it saved a fortune on premises. And made a second from the redevelopment of the old business districts into the new villages. The traders' quality of life had soared. Even the regulators were happy. Oh, they'd gone out of their minds, when the idea had first surfaced, he recalled with a broad grin. No control, impossible to manage risks properly, rogue traders would run rampant, a hacker's paradise, a disaster a day. They'd got quite poetic in their state of near apoplexy, particularly for that sub-human species. But in fact the security was far better than anything in the bad old days.

It was, he supposed, theoretically possible to get round the system. An impostor might get past it, if they could simultaneously match a registered user's voice, iris, finger and palm prints – and goodness knows how many other tests. There were rumors that it even constantly tested online traders against their DNA chain patterns. That might explain the compulsory blood – and highly embarrassing "other fluids" – samples that were part of the initial registration routine and the monthly "fit and proper" check-up.

No, security wasn't a problem. Only registered users could access the system and a trade wasn't recognized as even existing unless it passed through it.

But it was time to get to down to work. Which markets should he trade this morning? His fingers danced across the giant screen, flicking through the custom-built reports the system compiled for him whenever he was offline. This digital drudgery was a bit too much like hard work. The sooner they got those thought-recognition programs sorted out once and for all the better.

Still, at least he didn't have to waste any time thinking about which exchange he wanted to trade or whether the OTCs looked better. Oh no, GLOMART offered the whole caboodle – other than a few decidedly weird outfits who had been refused admittance. And no one in their right mind went near that stuff. A lot of the former exchanges still had a role, looking after and promoting certain contracts. But all that squabbling and criminal waste of time and money were things of the past. Now they had to concentrate on what mattered.

When GLOMART had first started, the exchanges had submitted their bids for the contracts they wanted to "own." They'd had to detail the amount they would pay towards the vast set-up costs, the trading fee they wanted to charge, and the percentage they would retain. The winners got a one-year exclusive on their contract.

Some exchanges had tried to buck the trend to start with, of course. But members' outrage, dwindling volumes, and deserted floors soon brought them to their senses. Quite a few of the dinosaurs had, thankfully, gone out of business.

The old OTCs went through a similar upheaval. Wild rumors of all sorts of unlikely parties and strange combinations had abounded for months. But, as usual, they were all wrong. The GLOMART shareholders – the banks, brokers, and multinationals – had simply formed a consortium and put in pre-emptive bids for the lot. Nothing was going to be allowed to spoil the start-up.

The fun had really started when that first year was over. Now any exchange or company – and even wealthy individuals – could introduce a new or competing contract. As long as they could pass the "fit and proper" tests and come up with the admission fee, "their" contract went on the system and off they went. If there was sufficient demand and the volume came their way, they got the income. Fortunes had been made and lost, but the variety of different types of deal that were now available had never been greater.

And with the ever increasing competition, those transaction fees just went down and down. As had the admission fee, now that GLOMART was well and truly tried, tested, and steaming along. The last time he'd run through the figures, you needed a new contract to do about 200,000 lots a month to break even, but it must be half that now.

Working for GoldBank was OK. They left him pretty much to his own devices as long as he met his profit targets, but his limits had been tightened again last month. And these days you couldn't exceed them, not for a second. The system just wouldn't validate a deal that would take you over. Maybe it was time to dust down those off-the-wall contracts he'd designed in idle moments and go independent.

The swaps looked interesting this morning. Perhaps it was time for some action. Still feeling a little nostalgic, Chuck ignored the screen and donned his helmet. It cost an extra 2000 bucks a month, but it was worth every penny. Punching up his choice of market, he let the sights, sounds, and smells of the "floor" wash over him.

Chuck's eyes skimmed round, settling into the scene.

He concentrated and lifted 500-worth of offers in the seven years, spreading his business between the other participants and the deliberately robot-like figure that represented the collective screen-based business.

The confirms and validates flashed up in front of his eyes in a second. They'd been talking about speeding it up for a long time now, but it was worth the wait. At least you knew that the trade had registered and passed or failed the GLOCLEAR and GLOREG requirements. Setting his alert, stop-loss, and take-profit parameters, Chuck wandered on over to exchange pleasantries with the friends and acquaintances who were loitering in the social zone. They were all agreed. The market was infinitely better than in the bad old days.

The savings that came from using GLOCLEAR more than compensated for having to put up security on the old OTC trades. Inter-bank credit risk only existed in the history books. Margins – reduced by state-of-the-art correlation software to the minimum required for the health of the system – were paid instantaneously. Thanks to the constant mark to markets, even variation margin changed hands real time. A fail caused the offending position to be closed out on the spot. Settlement risk had long since disappeared. GLOCLEAR simultaneously settled both sides of every transaction – and always had the margin cushion, should there be any problems.

GLOREG was every trader's dream. Now that GLOMART only permitted margined, within limits, professional trading – and GLOCLEAR had consigned that immeasurable hoary old chestnut of systemic risk to oblivion – the bureaucrats could concentrate on their proper objectives. Protecting retail interests and locking up the crooks.

One market, one clearing house, and one regulator for everything. Yes, this truly is a global market, Chuck mused – noting with satisfaction that his trade in the seven years was already showing a 25 million dollar profit. 25 million?! In ten minutes! Surely not …

Yeowch! What the hell was that stabbing pain in his ribs? "Shift, your ass, sucker" his partner cursed, punctuating each word with another vicious jab of her elbow. Oh great, he thought, as he groped for the blaring alarm and dragged himself out of bed. If he ran, he might just still make the 5.23 …

THE REVOLUTIONARY'S LEXICON

We offer this lexicon as our guide to a few key words and phrases that will come to dominate all discussion of the Capital Market Revolution.

Cognitive Elite Those who will thrive in the eye of and in the wake of the Capital Market Revolution. They are cosmopolitan and likely to feel equally at home on several continents.

Corpocracy Any organization, or nation, which is run largely with the best interests of large corporations in mind. Corpocracy in an age of dynamic and often microscopic companies was outmoded as soon as the Capital Market Revolution began, if not before …

Cyber Cash Electronic money, delivered by smart cards. When asset-backed they are known as ETUs (see below).

Derivative At once both an offshoot of modern finance but also (in the digital age) the hub around which all other markets gravitate. Literally, a product derived from a cash market.

Disintermediation The process of being bypassed by the food chain. Not a word to bandy around in front of nervous brokers or insecure exchange officials.

E-local An independent trader speculating regularly (usually intraday) on any of the world's major exchanges.

ETU Electronic Trading Units, i.e. cybercash. ETUs will probably be asset-backed by stock, securitized assets, or plain old-fashioned glittering resources, both precious metals and the fluid stuffs.

Ex-Dividend To be made redundant. Can also refer to corporations going bankrupt.

Facilitator Anybody who can still rightfully claim the right to intermediate. Trading-screen providers undoubtedly facilitate business; few brokers or exchanges will be able to claim to be facilitating business unless they can adapt to the New Reality with gusto.

Fiat money Bank notes that never held their value. Governments used to palm them off on citizens until ETUs stopped that sort of profligacy.

Free agent Any independent individuals who are operating beyond their national borders. Many e-locals epitomize the free agent spirit – working offshore, enjoying a more relaxed level of regulation, and quite probably existing tax-free.

Luddites The managers who reckon full service brokerage is not affected by online brokers; the exchange supremos who believe that open outcry is the only way to trade; the traders who want to phone their orders to their broker.

Microbanker The new, most dynamic form of digital banker. Operating with a tiny permanent executive, the small but perfectly formed microbankers will come to dominate much of the banking business on every level. A similar bounty awaits the microbroker, who will often be directly affiliated to the microbanker.

The New Reality "No one person or party's place in the trading chain is now assured."

NewVas New Value-Added Services: the process which brokers must embrace if they are to succeed in the New Reality. Remember: the old ways are the ways of the dead.

Reintermediation Believe it or not, there are actually some new forms of middle men who will emerge in the wake of the Capital Market Revolution. Those who can find such a niche will make a fortune, albeit on a high volume and microscopically thin margin basis.

Repudiation What every electronic broker and exchange fears … A trader does a deal and then claims it wasn't them. Repudiation risk can have a big potential impact on an exchange's morale and reputation, even when the market itself is vindicated. The Salomons "big swinging elbow" trade on MATIF ably demonstrated just how worrisome "repudiation" can be.

Smart card The lovely little bit of plastic that allows you to hold currency that is not necessarily issued by a government. A device that can produce money, allow you to make purchases, and – even better – give you access to your trading terminal in the quest for a few more cyberdollars.

Supercompetition The old markets looked competitive. Electronic markets raise competitive pressures to this even higher plane.

TOMBIS Total Online Investment Management By Individual Solutions. TOMBIS means individuals taking total control of their assets.

Throttling The process of orders being pressed into some sort of bottle-neck when they ought to be allowed to proceed freely. Typical examples of throttling includes insufficient bandwidth somewhere between an order being sent from the end-user terminal to the exchange, or a brokerage that has failed to grasp the Capital Market Revolution's central tenets and insists on placing some form of human intermediation in the path of an electronically transferred order.

Trading arcade A center in which traders operate *en masse*. Usually operated by an exchange affiliated clearing agent or a brokerage.

Virtual aliens Those guys doing your back-office paperwork and computer programming from New Delhi, India. They feel just like your colleagues in the New York office but in fact they are manifesting the global digital economy.

FURTHER READING FOR REVOLUTIONARIES

Bernstein, Peter L. (1996) *Against the Gods*, John Wiley.

Bryan, Lowell and Farrell, Diana (1996) *Marketing Unbound – Unleashing Global Capitalism*, John Wiley.

Carlson, Charles B. (1998) *The Individual Investor Revolution*, McGraw-Hill.

Chandler, Beverly (1998) *Investing with the Hedge Fund Giants – Profit Whether Markets Rise or Fall*, Financial Times Pitman Publishing.

Chernow, Ron (1997) *The Death of the Banker*, Pimlico.

Cobban, A. (1979) *A History of Modern France*, vol. 1 1715–1799, Penguin Books.

Cotton, Bob and Oliver, Richard (1997) *Understanding Hypermedia 2000*, Phaidon.

Dale Davidson, James and Rees-Mogg, William (1997) *The Sovereign Individual – The Coming Economic Revolution and How to Survive and Prosper in It*, Macmillan.

Dembo, Ron and Freeman, Andrew (1998) *Seeing Tomorrow – Rewriting the Rules of Risk*, John Wiley.

Hama, Noriko (1996) *Disintegrating Europe – The Twilight of the European Construction*, Adamantine Press.

Kelly, Kevin (1998) *New Rules for the New Economy – 10 Ways the Network Economy is Changing Everything*, Fourth Estate.

Leer, Anne (ed.) (1999) *Masters of the Wired World – Cyberspace Speaks Out*, Financial Times Pitman Publishing.

Lederman, Jess and Klein, Robert A. (eds) (1995) *Hedge Funds – Investment and Portfolio Strategies for the Institutional Investor*, Irwin Professional Publishing.

Melamend, Leo with Tamarkin, Bob (1996) *Escape to the Futures*, John Wiley.

Naisbitt, John (1996) *Global Paradox*, Allen and Unwin.

Tapscott, Don (1996) *The Digital Economy – Promise and Peril in the Age of Networked Intelligence*, McGraw-Hill.

Taylor, A.J.P. (1979) *Europe: Grandeur and Decline*, Penguin Books.

Von Hayek, Freidrich (1976) *The Denationalisation of Money*, The London Institute of Economic Affairs.

Periodicals

Applied Derivatives Trading www.adtrading.com

Business 2.0 www.business2.com

Forrester Research www.forrester.com

Fortune www.fortune.com

Institutional Investor www.iimagazine.com

MIT Technology Review www.techreview.com

The Economist www.economist.com

Financial Times www.ft.com

The Red Herring www.herring.com

Technology Review www.techreview.com

Wired www.wired.com

AMEX	American Exchange	LCH	London Clearing House
API	Open architecture protocol	LIFFE	London International Financial Futures and Options Exchange
APT	Automated Pit Trading		
ASX	Australian Stock Exchange	LTCM	Long Term Capital Management
ATP	Automated Trading Platform	MATIF	Marché à Terme International de France
BTP	Buoni del Tesore Poliennate (Italian Government Bonds)	MEFF	Mercado Español de Futures y Opciones Financieras
CAC	Cotation Assistée en Continu (superseded by the NSC)	MIF	Mercato Italiano dei Futures
		MONEP	Marché des Options Négociables de Paris
CBOE	Chicago Board Options Exchange	NASDAQ	National Association of Securities Dealers Automated Quotation
CBOT	Chicago Board of Trade		
CFTC	Commodities Futures Trading Commission	NSC	Nourean Systènie de Cotation
CME	Chicago Mercantile Exchange	NYSE	New York Stock Exchange
CTA	Commodity trading advisor	OMLX	OM London Exchange
DPO	Direct Public Offering	OTC	Over the counter
DTB	Deutsche Terminbörse	SBF	Société de Bourse Français
EMU	Economic and monetary union		
		SEC	Securities and Exchange Commission
ERM	Exchange Rate Mechanism	SFE	Sydney Futures Exchange
ETU	Electronic trading units	SIMEX	Singapore International Monetary Exchange
EUREX	European Exchange		
FIA	Futures Industry Association (US)	SOFFEX	Swiss Options and Financial Futures Exchange
FOA	Futures and Options Association (UK)		
		STIR	Short-term interest rate
GLOBEX	Global Exchange	TIFFE	Tokyo International Financial Futures Exchange
IPE	International Petroleum Exchange		
IPO	Initial public offering	TOMBIS	Total Online Investment Management By Individual Solutions
ISE	International Securities Exchange		
LAN	Local Area Network	VaR	Value at Risk